NORTH AMERICAN INDIANS

NORTH AMERICAN INDIANS

A Pictorial History of the Indian Tribes of North America

COLIN TAYLOR

SIENA

AUTHOR'S ACKNOWLEDGEMENTS

I have drawn gratefully on the extensive literature dealing with the North American Indian,
as well as on the results of my own researches over the past forty years.
I should like, therefore, to thank the following for their help and co-operation in many different ways:

Scott Bear Don't Walk, June and Erroll Bedford, Sam Cahoon, Richard Collins, Stu Connor,
Father Louis Cyr, S. J., John Day, Hugh Dempsey, Art Einhorn, Barbara Feezor-Stewart, Paula Fleming,
Terry Forshaw, Richard Gralewski, George Hamell, Bill Holm, Robert Mucci, George Horse Capture,
Heidi Howe, Mike Johnson, Dennis Lessard, S. D. Nelson, John Painter, Robert Penn and Robin Ridington.

My thanks also to Frances and Pedro Prá-Lopez of Kingfisher Design, London, who –
with great skill, consideration and ready comprehension – have carefully designed this volume.
I hope it will open up the rich and varied field of North American Indian culture to a wide audience.

Finally, once again, sincere thanks to my wife, Betty, who has – as with all my other research papers and
books on this fascinating subject – helped to create this volume and made my task so much easier.
In that respect, she is the co-author.

This is a Siena Book.
Siena is an imprint of Parragon.

First published in Great Britain in 1997 by Parragon
13 Whiteladies Road, Clifton, Bristol BS8 1PB

Copyright © 1997 Parragon

ISBN 0-75252-629-4
Printed in Italy

ACKNOWLEDGEMENTS

Produced by Kingfisher Design, London

Design and Project Director: Pedro Prá-Lopez

Typesetting and page formatting: Frances Prá-Lopez
Text Editors: Linda Doeser, Frances Prá-Lopez
Index: Linda Doeser
Maps: Mark Weaver
Colour Reprographics: Colour Quest Graphic Services, London

The paintings on the Half-title, Frontispeice and Title pages are all by Bill Holm.

Half-title page: A Plains Indian wearing a warbonnet with brow band decorated in the so-called lazy stitch and embellished with ermine. Typical of the period, *circa* 1880.

Frontispiece: Parade. Nez Perce woman and man (Plateau). The artist describes these Indians who 'in their finest dress and horsegear ride in the sun and dust to a celebration in the late nineteenth century'. Their costumes show considerable influence from the Crow Indians (Plains).

Title page: A Crow Indian wearing a magnificent shirt embellished with bands worked in the so-called quill-wrapped horsehair technique – a style worn by high-ranking Crow warriors in the period *circa* 1850–80. Although also found amongst the Nez Perce, the makers of the finest of this particular type of garment were probably the Mountain Crow.

CONTENTS

CULTURAL AREAS OF THE NORTH AMERICAN INDIAN

Numerals on the map denote the chapter number of the relevant cultural area

Description of North American Indian motifs used throughout the book

INTRODUCTION

There is little doubt that the Americas have been 'discovered' at least three, if not more, times. In about AD980, the Viking explorer, Eirik the Red, founded a large colony in Greenland which flourished for several hundred years. From here travels were made to present-day Newfoundland (which the Vikings called 'Vinland'), where smaller colonies were set up. Then, due to a combination of factors – climate, disease, privation and later war with the Eskimo – the colonies declined so that by the time Christopher Columbus reached the New World in 1492, the Norsemen had gone. Whilst the indigenous populations do not figure in the early Norse records, they were prominent in those of Columbus. He reported in February 1493 that when he had landed on the shores of San Salvador, several months before, he believed that he had landed in the East Indies and had encountered the *Idios*. As a result of his error, the indigenous inhabitants of North America are now universally designated as American Indians – descendants of peoples who had reached the New World from Asia, aeons before either the Vikings or Columbus.

For two prolonged periods between *circa* 37,000BC and 30,000BC, and again between 26,000BC and 11,000BC, massive glaciers covered great areas of Siberia, present-day Alaska and Canada. With so much water locked up in ice and snow, sea levels dropped, exposing land and linking the Old to the New World. It was via this land-bridge – now referred to as Beringia (after the Danish explorer, Vitus Bering) that *Homo sapiens* – 'modern' man – as well as animals and plants, first reached North America. Now referred to as the *Paleo-Indian* period, the people were big-game

◀ *Talking Wall* (*circa* 1993), by the Standing Rock Sioux artist S.D. Nelson, who is also a commercial artist and designer. The painting shows the ancient Anasazi pictographs in the 'forgotten' canyons of Arizona, rediscovered by S.D. who observed: 'These images spoke to me across the ages in a clear voice that made my heart cry … the rock art of the ancient ones, my ancestors'.

hunters who, armed with flint-headed spears (the bow and arrow was yet to be imported) could bring down outsize bison, American horses and most importantly, mammoths. It was a lifestyle which extended on both American subcontinents until about 6,000BC, by which time, both mammoth and mastodon were extinct.

The shaping of the American Indian

The demise of the mammoth saw the gradual passing of the Paleo-Indian. Slowly, by tiny changes in behaviour new traits were adopted giving rise to a more sophisticated culture. This *Archaic* period saw exploitation of a variety of food resources demanding not only new patterns of living, but new ideas and greater ingenuity. It set the scene for the so-called *Formative* period, which began about 1,000BC (roughly coinciding with the introduction of corn from the Southwest) and extended to AD1,000. It was a time during which most of the cultural areas north of Mexico, discussed in this book, were being consolidated.

Despite the diversity between cultural areas, there were several elements which were common throughout North America. Spirituality was important, together with a recognition of the great forces of nature and the universe. This was interwoven in a mysticism which put importance on dreams, shamans and animal powers. On a

more practical level, there was great emphasis on inter-tribal trading well down into Mexico.

Arts and crafts were also a prime concern, great ingenuity and skill being shown in the production of clothing, utensils, habitations, religious and ceremonial objects and devices for transportation. Many cultural areas were highly democratic, the power of leaders being limited by both council and the opinions of the elders. Most American Indian

▲ A superb Seminole shoulder bag dating from *circa* 1840. At this time both Seminole and Creek men wore pouches supported by broad straps, as shown here. Usually decorated with very small seed beads, they closely resembled those worn by Scottish Highlanders. Research has revealed some seven thousand gold-plated beads on this bag – little wonder that such items were worn as status symbols!

Two Chiricahua Apache warriors (*above left*). The man on the left is Chato, of high rank and a close associate of Geronimo. Like the Navajo, the Apache were relative newcomers to the Southwest and the Chiricahua sub-tribe were true desert and mountain dwellers.

▶ To supplement income, Iroquois women produced beaded items which they sold to tourists – a major outlet being Victoria Falls. These 'whimsies' were very popular in Victorian times.

leaders excelled at speech-making, knew the effectiveness and impact of good communication skills and were clever negotiators.

These common elements aside, it is really only within the cultural areas that shared patterns of lifestyle and ceremonial are seen and, even here, there were often variations between tribes.

At the time of Columbus, the indigenous population probably did not exceed two million. There were at least six parent linguistic stocks, with some five hundred different languages. This necessitated the use of a sophisticated sign language which was widely used and understood.

Environmental factors played a crucial role in shaping the destiny and lifestyle of the indigenous inhabitants. In some areas of the Southeast, but particularly along the Northwest Coast, the people depended predominantly on the sea and rivers for their subsistence, generally living a settled life. In the fertile lands of the East, Midwest and, to a lesser extent, the Southwest, the emphasis was on horticulture, but here also they lived a settled life. Most such lifestyles were clearly established at the time of Columbus' discovery. One notable exception was the Great Plains. A difficult terrain it was to see a variety of peoples come and go. It was not until the horse filtered up from the Spanish colonies in the Southwest that the dynamic equestrian culture emerged (*see Chapter 1*).

The changing face of America

Columbus was much impressed and charmed with '*Los Idios*' and wrote to his sponsors, the King and Queen of Spain: 'So tractable, so peaceful are these people, that I swear to your Majesties there is not a better nation on earth ...' There was, however, a further and more sinister message from Columbus – the docile *Idios*, he promised, could be sent back as slaves, whilst others might be 'made to work, sow and do all that is necessary and to adopt our ways' – sentiments, particularly the last, which would be echoed by Europeans over the next four centuries!

After Columbus, came Spanish slave traders under Ponce de León, raiding the Florida coast and attempting to capture the Calusa and Timucua, ancient inhabitants of the region. Although fierce and determined fighters the majority were driven from the mainland by the late eighteenth century.

The gold-finding expeditions of de Soto and Coronado in the 1540s penetrated as far as what is now Arkansas. Seeking the city of Quivira, which was believed to be of great wealth, they were disappointed, killed their treacherous guide 'The Turk' and before returning home also killed the Indians, burnt crops and captured their leaders.

This pattern was replicated by the French, Dutch and English – initial amicable exchanges turning, as interests clashed, into unimaginable ferocity on both sides. Indian populations

▶ Frog bowl carved from alder wood, Tlingit, probably Sitka and dating from *circa* 1880. Such vessels were orginally used in feasts to hold seal or fish oil which was seved with various foods. It is a higly imaginative piece, deeply embedded in Northwest Coast traditions, one scholar commenting, 'This whimsical frog image illustrates a bowl-frog that has come dramatically to life ... and lifts itself up as if looking at and testing the air in its new territory'.

▲ 'Struck-by-The-Ree' a Yankton Sioux and Barbara Feezor-Stewart's (*see page 92*) great-great-grandfather, photographed in 1872.

plummeted as *Massasoit*, chief of the Wampanoags (of present-day Rhode Island), observed on signing a treaty in the 1630s: 'Englishmen, take [the] land, for none is left to occupy it'.

Noting the destruction and fearful for the future, leaders such as *Powhatan* and his brother *Opechancanough*, put up fierce opposition to the colonization of Virginia by the English in the 1630s. Later, *Metacomet* of the Wampanoags (*circa* 1670) and Shawnee leader, *Tecumseh* (*circa* 1812), travelled widely in an attempt to unite the tribes – to no avail.

So it continued from the Atlantic to the Pacific: the 'Manifest Destiny' of America and with it the inevitable, progressive destruction of its indigenous peoples ... little wonder, as one American Indian scholar later observed, 'Custer died for your sins'.

The westward expansion: a clash of cultures

By 1800, the frontier was expanding rapidly with further impetus to westward expansion – a vast process of migration and settlement referred to as Manifest Destiny, whose architect was Thomas Jefferson, third President of the United States. As one historian has observed, however, '[it] brought manifest disaster to the Indians'.

The Lewis and Clark expedition (1803–1806) set up to survey Louisiana was, with one notable exception, received with the same eagerness and warmth that had greeted most earlier European

▲ *Wapella*, headman of the Mesquakie or Fox tribe of Wisconsin, who referred to themselves as the 'Red Earth People'.

◄ Frosted, a Sioux medicine man, in chains. Photographed by pioneer photographer D.F. Barry, *circa* 1890.

▼ Cheyenne Indians and their interpreter, John Smith, at Fort Leavenworth, Kansas in 1863.

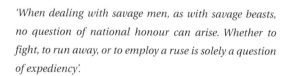

explorers. Peace Medals – the image of Jefferson on one side and clasped hands and pipes on the other – were issued to Indian leaders as a sign of friendship. The message from Jefferson was an honourable one and delivered by honourable men, but before the end of the decade, smallpox, alcohol and conflict began to take their toll on the western tribes.

War with the Plains Indians all began with a cow so thin and emaciated it had been abandoned by its Mormon emigrant owner on the Oregon Trail. On the afternoon of 18 August, 1854, High Forehead, a Miniconjou Sioux, desiring a piece of rawhide and perhaps a questionable meal into the bargain, shot the cow dead. Demanding compensation, Lieutenant John Grattan, with thirty-odd men, rode into the Sioux camp: Conquering Bear, Man Afraid of Horses and other headmen appealed for reason, but it was not to be. Shots were fired, Conquering Bear fell mortally wounded and within minutes, Grattan and all but one of his men were dead. The episode heralded a slow war of suppression on the Plains, Plateau and beyond to California, which was to last nearly forty years.

'When dealing with savage men, as with savage beasts, no question of national honour can arise. Whether to fight, to run away, or to employ a ruse is solely a question of expediency'.

General Francis C. Walker, Commissioner of Indian Affairs. *Circa* 1875.

A new deal for the First Americans

Through the 1870s and early 1880s, there were disturbances across the Plains and beyond. In 1874 gold was discovered in the Black Hills, sacred territory of the Sioux, which led to a rush of gold-seekers. Offered six million dollars for the Hills, the Sioux refused and demanded seventy million. Frustrated, the government ordered the Indians to the reservation agencies and if they refused, they were to be treated as hostiles – few complied! So arose the last great battles for the West – Rosebud (1876) when Crook with one thousand men was outmanoeuvred by Crazy Horse's forces; Custer and his immediate command annihilated on the Little Bighorn eight days later (1876); the epic retreat of Joseph's Nez Perce to Canada (1877); the Ute wars of 1879; the Apache wars of the 1880s and finally, Wounded Knee in December 1890.

The long fight of the First Americans was over. Confined to reservations, the tribes languished for almost two generations, a forgotten, abused and exploited people. An effort to dispossess the Pueblo of their ancient tribal lands in the 1920s drew attention to the appalling conditions prevailing on the reservations and led to the Merrian Report of 1928 which suggested urgent matters to improve conditions. The Indian Reorganization Act of 1934, passed by President Roosevelt, saw a shift in the government's attitude. It provided for a degree of

▲ *Victory at the Little Bighorn*, by Standing Rock Sioux artist, S. D. Nelson, *circa* 1993. S.D's caption for this painting (his is work much inspired by the Sioux historian, Amos Bad Heart Bull), read, 'As a boy, I was taught that there were no survivors at the battle of the Little Bighorn. However, that was merely the white man's account. There were hundreds of Lakota and Cheyenne who lived to tell the story of their struggle and victory'.

◄ Charles Red Cloud, grandson of the famous Oglala Sioux chief, *Makhpiya-lúta*, who fought valiantly and then diplomatically for tribal lands in the last quarter of the nineteenth century. A staunch traditionalist, Charles insisted on putting on his warbonnet before this photograph was taken on the Pine Ridge Reservation in South Dakota in 1966.

tribal self-government and made funds available to develop schools, hospitals and cultural amenities. This represented the beginning of a series of initiatives to improve the material quality of life of the American Indians, which reached its height during the Kennedy and Johnson administrations. These 1960's policies were reversed during the Reagan administration to encourage closer integration with mainstream American culture, edicts which continue under President Bill Clinton.

American Indians now face a new revolution – the end of the reservation system which has governed their lives for more than a century. This has forced many tribes to begin to explore the possibilities of a new life beyond government dependency. American Indian scholars, artists and writers are increasingly demonstrating that their culture and innovative spirit has much to offer, such as the artwork of S.D. Nelson, Robert Penn, Arthur Amiotte and Wilmer Dupree; the poetry of Wendy Rose a Hopi/Miwok; the story-telling of the tribal historian, Joseph Medicine Crow, to name a few (*see Chapter 10*). As George Horse Capture, Deputy Assistant Director for Cultural Resources at the new National Museum of the American Indian (N.M.A.I.), has observed, 'the future of the Native American people lies in a renewed understanding of the old ways… and re-establishing a continuity between the present and the past.'

THE GREAT PLAINS: A LAND OF SUN, WIND AND GRASS

People of the buffalo

The Great Plains is the vast heartland of North America, stretching from northern Alberta, south into Texas, a distance of some two thousand miles (3,220km). To the east, its border is approximately the Missouri-Mississippi valleys and to the west, the foothills of the Rocky Mountains. In total the Great Plains encompasses an area of some one million square miles (about 2.6m sq km). Although one main feature is a level surface of great extent, it is a land of tremendous contrasts, both in climate and terrain. To the south and west, the limited rainfall produces a semi-desert-like terrain, whilst in the Missouri and Mississippi valleys, the higher rainfall gives green prairies and, at times, humid conditions. Some regions are renowned for their beauty, particularly in the river valleys where there are lush grasses, outcrops of timber and, in the historic period, abundant wildlife.

Vast herds of buffalo and antelope roamed the Great Plains in the historic period. Conservative estimates give a figure of more than sixty million buffalo in the early nineteenth century and it is likely that the antelope population at this time was comparable. The latter, more fully described as a

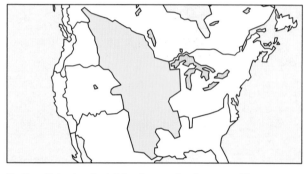

The Great Plains, heartland of America, covering almost one million square miles and home to the 'typical' Indian – Blackfeet, Sioux, Cheyenne and Kiowa.

prong-horned antelope because of the peculiar shape of its horns, exemplifies the characteristics of most Plains animals – able to survive without water for lengthy periods, ultra cautious, having a keen sense of smell and extremely difficult to approach. Classed as the purest type of Plains animal, the pronghorn is amongst the swiftest animals in the world, communicating over great distances using a flare of white on its rump.

◀ The *Mauvais Terre* or 'Badlands' territory of the Plains Sioux in present-day South Dakota. It was to this area that the Miniconjou Sioux leader, Big Foot, retreated after the killing of Sitting Bull in December 1890. As can be seen here, this is a barren, rugged and hostile region where temperatures can fluctuate dramatically.

The people

The historic Plains Indians – those people who inhabited the Great Plains in the eighteenth and nineteenth centuries – belong to several different linguistic families. Dominant was Algonquian and Siouan but Athapaskan, Caddoan and Uto-Aztecan was also spoken by some tribes. Languages differed considerably even within the same linguistic family, for example the Cree and Blackfeet were both Algonquian speakers but they could not understand one another.

Over thirty tribes shared a sufficient number of similar traits to classify them as Plains Indians. To the west were the Nez Perce and Shoshone who, although generally classified as Plateau peoples, made frequent forays into the Plains region. To the east were tribes, sometimes described as the Prairie tribes, who practised some horticulture and lived in permanent villages and whose culture was a mixture of Plains and Woodland. The main tribes in the north, occupying regions which are now Alberta, Saskatchewan and northern Montana, were the Cree, Blackfeet and Assiniboin. On the Central Plains in present-day North and South Dakota, Nebraska, Wyoming and Montana, were the Sioux, Cheyenne, Arapaho, Crow, Mandan, Hidatsa and Arikara, whilst the Southern Plains in what is now Colorado, Kansas and Oklahoma, were dominated by the Kiowa and Comanche.

▲ The Platte River near Fort Laramie in Wyoming. The domain of the Plains Indian was a land of sun, wind and grass, with regions of great beauty and richness. The tipi villages were generally to be found in such areas, the best sites being well known to the indigenous inhabitants.

Physical appearance

While tribal appearance was largely influenced by methods of dressing the hair, general posture and costume, there were some physical differences. Faces of the northern tribes, such as the Cree, Assiniboin and Blackfeet, were often rather rounded and almost delicate, whilst those of the Pawnee and Omaha were large and heavy. The Sioux and Cheyenne had long faces, clear-cut features, an eagle nose and prominent cheek bones. Stature too varied somewhat from one tribe to the next; the male, adult Cheyenne – tallest of the Plains Indians – averaged 68.7 inches (1.745m), the Blackfeet 67.5 inches (1.715m), the Arikara 66.5 inches (1.69m). In general, at the time measurements were made in the early nineteenth century, the Indians of the Great Plains were a tall people, compared with other Indians and mankind as a whole.

Considering the enormous impact that the Plains Indian image has had on the perception of the North American Indian, the total population was surprisingly low, probably never exceeding more than 150,000. Likewise, tribal numbers were modest; that of the Blackfeet, amongst the largest of the tribes – has been estimated at 15,000 in 1780, whilst the Plains Sioux numbered 10,000 at about the same time.

▲ The Blackfeet medicine man, Lazy Boy, photographed in 1947. A prominent leader in the Sun Dance ceremonials, he typifies the traits of several tribes on the Northern Plains, whom the anthropologist Clark Wissler, described as having rather rounded and delicate features.

▲ The Hunkpapa Sioux warrior, Running Antelope, photographed in Washington in 1872. He wears a beautiful shirt embellished with porcupine quills, fringed with hair and carries a fan made from an eagle's wing and a long pipe with a bowl made of soft catlinite stone.

The sign language and winter counts

Because of the diversity of languages, an ingenious sign language was developed which was understood throughout the region and beyond. It was invaluable for effective communication in the complex inter-tribal trade network which was a vital component of the Plains Indian way of life.

With no formal written language, tribal history and other important events were recorded using ingenious pictographs, the most impressive being the so-called 'Winter Counts', which were particularly well developed by the Sioux and Kiowa.

Lifestyle

The key traits of Plains Indian culture were a dependence on the buffalo, limited use of berries and roots, absence of fishing and agriculture and the use of the tipi as a movable dwelling. Transportation was by land only, using a *travois*, an

▲ Distribution of Plains tribes, *circa* 1850 (after Clark Wissler, 1920). The ranges of the various tribes are approximately indicated by the positions and extent of their respective names. The typical Plains tribes are those designated by an asterisk.

Winter counts

Amongst several of the Plains Indian tribes, but in particular the Sioux and Kiowa, there were tribal historians who kept a record of tribal history and important events using pictographic symbols. These were referred to by the Sioux as *waniyétü wowápi*, 'winter record' or *waniyétü yawápi*, 'winter count' and it is from the latter that the English name is derived. The main function of these winter counts seems to have been to preserve important events for the instruction of future generations, but they were also used as calendars – keeping track of the passage of years and noting the number of years between one memorable event and another.

Although lacking a written language, an individual could refer to his band's winter count to ascertain, if he was not sure, how old he was. Additional information might be needed, for example that he was born in the winter, 'The stars showered down' (1833); then the Keeper of the Count, having found this reference point on the *waniyétü yawápi*, could count the number of pictographs after this event and so was able to determine the individual's exact age.

On the calendar shown here, which is the famous 'Lone Dog Winter Count', the pictographs are arranged spirally and read from the centre working anti-clockwise. The first pictograph refers to thirty Sioux killed by Crow Indians in the year 1800–01, the second to a smallpox outbreak (1801–02), whilst the spectacular meteor showers of 1833–4 are depicted top left.

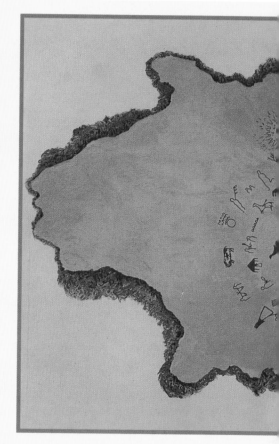

A-shaped sled, which was pulled by a dog or horse. Basketry, pottery and weaving were limited or absent altogether. Clothing was of buffalo- and deerskins and containers were of rawhide. Work in stone, wood or bone was limited. Much of the artwork was geometrical with superb products,

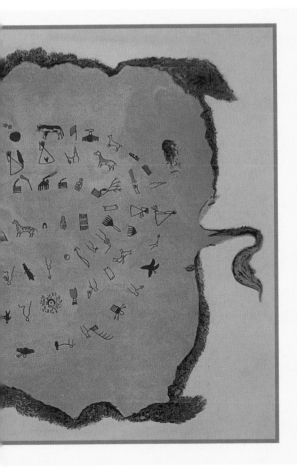

such as clothing, tipi accoutrements, society regalia and horse equipment being decorated with painting, porcupine quillwork or beads.

Tribes were mostly composed of relatively independent units under the leadership of a chief, supported by a number of headmen. The complexity of tribal organization and the relationship between various units differed considerably, but when the disparate units came together for annual gatherings there was a well-defined camp circle organization.

Another feature of Plains culture was the existence of a series of societies for both men and women as well as several major, annual ceremonials, the most prominent of which was the Sun Dance.

However, not all tribes adhered to this broad pattern. For example, the Missouri River tribes, such as the Mandan, Hidatsa, Arikara, Omaha and Pawnee, lived in semi-permanent villages with earth lodge habitations and their most important ceremonials differed markedly from the Sun Dance. For example, the annual Pawnee Morning Star ceremonial put great emphasis on astronomical phenomena and even performed human sacrifice; while that of the Mandan *O-kee-pa*, stressed their dependence on the buffalo – although there were certain aspects of this ritual which suggest a link with the Sun Dance.

▲ A Plains Indian *travois*. On the march, most tribes used this A-shaped type of sled, the baggage being placed on an oval or (as shown here), rectangular platform. Tipi covers made of hide (*below*) and weighing as much as 100lbs (45kg) could be carried relatively easily this way, as could passengers, who were protected from falling off by a cage made of crossed sticks. Smaller *travois* were also used; pulled by dogs, they relieved the women of the burden of transporting firewood.

▲ Typical hide tipis of the Plains tribes. Such portable dwellings were made of twelve or more buffalo hides which were carefully tanned, trimmed and then sewn together into a semi-circular shaped cover. This was stretched across a conical frame made of eighteen or twenty long pine or cedar poles. Note the ear-like smoke flaps which could be adjusted to ensure good ventilation.

The earth lodge

The tipi was not the only type of shelter used by the Plains Indians. Tribes such as the Mandan, Hidatsa and Arikara – as well as the Pawnee and Omaha farther down the Missouri River – lived in semi-permanent villages in dome-shaped, earth-covered lodges.

A typical earth lodge had a frame of some ten to fifteen stout posts set up in a circle. Beams were then laid across the tops of these posts extending from one to another. Near the centre of the lodge, four more longer posts were set into the ground forming a square of about fifteen feet (4.5m) and their tops were connected with beams laid horizontally. Long poles, as rafters, were now put in place with willow saplings woven between them. The whole frame was then covered with a thick layer of hay and earth, the entrance being via a short passageway (as can be seen in the illustration *below left*). The fireplace was a circular depression at the centre of the lodge with a surround of flat rocks. Such habitations housed entire families, including elderly parents and even the favourite horses and dogs!

The earth lodge was comfortable, light and airy being well furnished with beds, backrests and screens to exclude draughts. The family's belongings, such as shields, lances and paddles, as well as household utensils, were hung or stacked around the interior (*below right*). The earth lodge was all but abandoned by the early twentieth century but they were a symbol of the good early days, as one elderly Hidatsa woman reminisced in 1908, 'when we used them we were healthy and there were many children and old people'.

▲ Mandan earth lodge showing the central village shrine. The entrance to the earth lodge was through a short passage.

▲ Mandan earth lodge interior, after a painting by Karl Bodmer (1834). The hole in the roof of the lodge allowed smoke to escape and light to enter.

Plains Indian religion

Living on the wide, open Plains, the tribes were in such daily communication with their environment and so dependent upon it, that much around them was considered to have a spiritual existence. There was a belief in a great controlling power, together with a series of lesser powers, which pervaded the universe; this was quite distinct from physical power and could act in different ways for good or evil. The Plains Sioux (Lakota) recognized a hierarchy of powers which they referred to as *Wakan-Tanka*, 'the sacred ones'. Four of the most important of these *wakan* beings, were *Wi*, the 'sun', *Skan*, 'sky' or 'energy', *Maka*, the 'earth' and *Inyan*, 'rock'. Next came the kindred *wakan* – Moon, Wind, White Buffalo Maiden and the Thunderbeings. In total, there were sixteen of these mysterious powers, each being grouped in fours and referred to as the *Tobtob Kin* – 'the four times four'.

Whilst the religious concepts of other Plains tribes have not been analysed in such depth as the Sioux, concepts of supernatural powers were similar. For example the Omaha *Wakonda*, Pawnee *Tirawahat* and Blackfeet *Natojewa*, may all be translated as 'the sacred ones'. It was against this background of religion that most ceremonial and ritual of the Plains Indian was set, the emphasis being on the harnessing of this power both at the tribal and individual level, to the very best effect.

The establishment of a rapport with the divine elements to gain supernatural help was the aim of all Plains Indian males, for it could ensure success in all activities and enhance an individual's social standing. Communication was established via the so-called Vision Quest, a youth putting himself in the hands of a powerful shaman who instructed him to retreat, in seclusion, for several days and nights. He would fast and pray, calling upon the mythical creatures, heavenly bodies and those on the waters and earth to give him a revelation. The dream or vision was, in turn, more fully interpreted by the shaman with subsequent conferment of

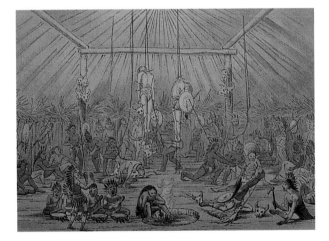

▲ An episode in the *O-kee-pa* ceremonial of the Mandan, depicted by the artist and traveller, George Catlin, who travelled amongst the Plains tribes in the 1830s. This depicts the interior of the Medicine Lodge during one of the more spectacular parts of the ceremonial, when penitents were suspended from the lodge beams by rawhide thongs through their breasts or backs.

The Sun Dance

The Sun Dance was one of the most important tribal events of several of the nomadic Plains tribes. The name is probably derived from the Sioux who speak of a part of the ceremonial as 'sun gazing', when the devotee gazes steadily at the sun while dancing.

One component of the Sun Dance involves an episode of torture where skewers pierce the breast (sometimes the back) and the worshipper appeals to the sun for divine guidance (*right*), while blowing on a whistle made of the wing bone of an eagle (*far right*). In this respect the Sun Dance of the nomadic Plains tribes is similar to the *O-kee-pa* ceremony of the Mandan (*left*) and it is possible that the two ceremonials are related.

Another important feature of the Sun Dance is that the tree used for the central pole, to which the

dancers were tied, was cut and felled as if conquering an enemy. After trimming and painting it was erected with great ceremonial. Various offerings were placed on it, a large bunch of twigs at the top symbolizing a Thunderbird's nest.

Traditionally, the time of the Sun

Dance was mid-summer. It was initiated by an individual who, at a time of stress or great danger, had made a vow to host the event. It was an opportunity for great tribal gatherings when, after the Sun Dance was over, the societies put on their own rituals and ceremonials.

▲ During the torture the participant blows on a whistle made of the wing bone of an eagle.
◄ The Sun Dance involves an episode of torture when skewers are used to pierce the worshipper's breast and sometimes the back.

sacred, 'medicine' songs and the designation of some object – skin, shell, feather, claw – to be carried and used as a charm or personal medicine bundle. In addition, there might be the commitment to some strange, formal taboos. Warriors of the Plains carried these charms into

battle, turning to them in times of stress as a source of supernatural aid. All associated obligations were strictly observed, be it a song, prayer or abstinence, for if violated, the power could be lost.

Most tribes also had much more pretentious bundles, which were used in connection only with complex ceremonials. Owned by high-ranking individuals or looked after by tribal societies they contained a variety of objects: pipes, stuffed animal skins, ears of maize, pieces of wood or stone, as well as items for use in the ceremonials. Emphasis was placed on the pipe as a ritual object, the rising smoke suggesting communication with the higher powers.

Famous bundles in this class included the Buffalo Calf Pipe bundle of the Plains Sioux; the Medicine Pipe bundles of the Blackfeet and Cree; the four Medicine Arrows of the Cheyenne; the Sacred Wheel and Pipe of the Arapaho and the *O-kee-pa* drums of the Mandan. Their contents and rituals were used to evoke the powers of the supernatural forces, initiating actions which played out tribal legends and mythology so ensuring the ethos and culture of the tribe were perpetuated.

◄ A small Cree Indian medicine bundle, probably used in healing rituals. The Cree were well known for their powerful medicine bundles which contained sacred objects to be used in any serious undertaking requiring the support of the higher powers. Some Christian influence is suggested here by the small cross adjacent to the horn and the small pieces of oddly-shaped wood.

The coming of the horse

Prior to the introduction of the horse by the Spaniards in the 1540s the inhabitants of the Great Plains led a pedestrian, nomadic existence. As the horse spread from the south, by trade or capture, Plains culture flowered. Some ancient occupants of the Northern Plains, such as the Shoshone and Kutenai, were gradually driven out as more powerful and now gun-carrying Blackfeet and others tribes pushed in from the north and east, motivated by the knowledge that a vast, rich domain would be theirs, if the gun and horse could be combined. Similarly, on the Southern Plains the horse-wealthy Comanche, with guns obtained from French allies, forced the Padouca off the Plains of Texas.

Although influenced by the Spanish, a distinctive Plains style of saddle, bridle, martingale and stirrup emerged, beautifully decorated with porcupine quills and beads; some of the finest women's horse accoutrements were made by the Crow.

The effects of the horse on the Plains people were profound. Using the larger, horse-drawn *travois* with its load-carrying platform, tipi covers and furnishings could be transported, more possessions acquired and greater distances travelled. More than anything, however, the vast herds of buffalo, offering plenty and prosperity, became readily accessible and relatively easy game.

▲ The Crow warrior, 'He-who-jumps-over-everyone'. A chromolithograph by George Catlin who met this man on the Upper Missouri in 1832. Catlin describes him as having long hair which 'almost reached the ground' and a 'profusely' decorated costume.

▼ A beautifully quilled headstall, probably Cree or Metis and dating from *circa* 1830. Such exquisite pieces, together with other types of horse equipment, were important commodities in the complex web of inter-tribal trade across the Plains.

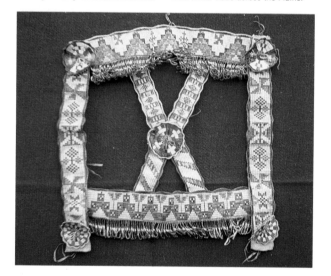

The buffalo

Vegetable foods were important in the Plains Indian's diet. Indeed, several of the groups on the Missouri – such as the Mandan, Hidatsa and Arikara – cultivated maize and those farther east – such as the Santee Sioux and Iowa – harvested wild rice. Wild fruits, seeds, nuts and roots, such as the prairie turnip, were also seasonally gathered.

Antelope, deer and elk were eaten, but buffalo meat was the staple diet of the Plains Indian. Buffalo also provided hides for clothing, dwellings and containers, and its horns, bones, hair and sinews provided the raw materials for a variety of arts and crafts.

▲ The most important of the Plains animals was the buffalo (*Bison americanus*) which roamed in vast herds. A bull buffalo, as shown here, stood almost 6½ feet (2m) at the shoulder and weighed 2,000lbs (about 900kg). The buffalo supplied almost all of the needs of the Plains people – primarily food and clothing – and its virtual extermination in the mid-1880s was the death knell of their entire culture.

The white buffalo

The buffalo was honoured by all Plains Indians as the wisest and most powerful of all creatures. It figured prominently in both Plains mythology and religion as a symbol of long life, plenty and leadership. The most revered, however, was the white buffalo and several tribes, such as the Sioux and Mandan, had mythology or ceremonials in which the white buffalo figured prominently. In the Mandan White Buffalo Cow Society, the leader wore a carefully tanned white buffalo robe. The rituals of this society centred around calling the buffalo into the vicinity of the village. White buffalo robes were also donated by the Mandan as offerings to the higher powers and were hung on poles adjacent to the *O-kee-pa* earth lodge.

When a white buffalo was slain, several actions were taken so as not to offend the spirits. The Sioux, for example, purified the fatal arrow in the smoke of burning sweetgrass, the knife used to skin the buffalo being likewise purified and great care was taken to remove the hide so that no blood was shed on the fur. Further, the woman who tanned the hide had to be one who was distinguished by the purity of her lifestyle and only men who had dreamed of animals were allowed to eat the flesh.

White buffalos are exceedingly rare – perhaps one in a million. Indeed, it is said amongst the traditional Lakota (Plains Sioux), that a white buffalo calf is born only every fourth generation, the calf coming during times of turmoil, famine and sickness. In recent years, one of the best-known white buffalo was 'Big Medicine' (shown here) who was born in May 1933 at the National Bison Range in Moiese, Montana. He was completely white except for a brown topknot between his horns and he had blue eyes. 'Big Medicine' died in August 1959. Another white buffalo which has recently received much attention was born on 20 August, 1994, on a small farm in Janesville, Wisconsin. Of great significance to contemporary Plains Indians, this calf has been given the name 'Miracle'.

▲ The white buffalo called 'Big Medicine'. Born in May 1933 in Moiese, Montana he died in 1959.

Prior to the introduction of the horse and firearms buffalo were hunted using special pounds which varied depending on the type of terrain. All were V-shaped and fenced with rocks or timber, the barrier extending for over a mile across the prairie. Buffalo were lured or driven into the entrance by 'buffalo callers' and then, panicked by the shouts and blanket-waving of the hunters previously concealed behind the barriers, were moved to the narrow end of the pound. This ended in a corral, with a drop of several feet, so maiming most of the animals as they fell. Other pounds ended at a cliff edge; if high, the buffalo sustained serious injury or death, if low, there was a corral at the base to prevent their escape. The 'buffalo jump', which depended on inter-band organization, was an effective way of securing a good supply of meat.

The arrival of the horse changed buffalo-hunting techniques. The favourite methods were the 'surround' or 'chase'. In the 'surround', the herd was milled into a frightened, galloping circle and the choice animals shot at close range from the saddle. In the less dangerous 'chase' a skirmish line of hunters, mounted on their favourite 'buffalo runners', slowly approached the herd; as the buffalo became aware of the intruders and started to move away, the hunters charged, each singling out one animal for the kill, which after a lengthy chase was despatched with bow, lance or gun.

▲ Various methods for hunting buffalo – the pound, surround or chase – demanded co-ordination and co-operation between the hunters. This technique, the 'still hunt', with the hunters dressed in wolf skins, was later copied by whites using guns. It required great stealth and patience. Wolves followed the buffalo herds and were a danger only to weak or young animals. Healthy buffalo were not intimidated by them.

Accidents were common – horses stumbled, guns misfired or exploded – and men were sometimes gored by a wounded buffalo. Dead buffalo were prepared for transportation to the village, the butchering generally being done by the women. If a white buffalo was slaughtered it was considered a most sacred animal and careful steps were taken so as not to offend the higher powers (*see page 19*).

In the late nineteenth century, buffalo-hunting became a sport and source of income to white explorers and hide hunters and many buffalo were slaughtered, so that by 1884 only a few hundred remained. Their virtual extermination was to signal the end of the historic Plains Indian culture.

Weapons and warpaint

Plains warriors went to war for personal prestige and glory, the capture of horses or simple revenge. A man who captured many horses gained status by giving the majority away to poorer people, but the greatest prestige came from the gaining of war honours or *coups* which put emphasis on touching a live enemy with the bare hand or a stick, rather than actually killing him. Other exploits, such as stealing a horse picketed outside the owner's tipi, capturing a gun, touching a dead enemy or taking a scalp, all led to the increased status of an individual who could then publicly recite such deeds at feasts and ceremonials and wear special regalia signifying his achievements and standing.

Weapons were the bow and arrow, stone-headed warclubs and shields. Later, a favoured trade item was the metal pipe tomahawk which combined both weapon and pipe in one unit. War parties out to capture enemy horses generally left the home camp on foot carrying extra moccasins and rations of pemmican (cakes of dried meat and berries). War regalia was packed into special rawhide containers often beautifully decorated with painted geometric designs. This regalia was worn by the successful returning party who made a ceremonial entry into the village, followed by gift giving, the reciting of the exploits and the performance of the scalp dance by the women.

▲ Four Bears or *Mato-tope*, the Mandan chief after a portrait *circa* 1834 painted by the Swiss artist, Karl Bodmer. *Mato-tope* was a man of outstanding leadership and military prowess. As shown here his hair ornaments depict both achievements and wounds sustained in battles with enemy tribes. He is carrying a war axe of a type popular in the middle-Missouri region at this time.

The scalp

Scalps were taken as war trophies by most Plains tribes. The portion taken was usually a small circular patch of skin at the root of the 'scalp-lock', just at the crown of the head. The scalp-lock itself was a small hair braid which hung from the back of the head as distinguished from the larger braids at the side of the head. This scalp-lock was often decorated with various ornaments, including feathers.

The operation of scalping was performed by making a quick knife stroke around the head of the disabled enemy followed by a strong tug on the scalp-lock. The individual who took the scalp was not necessarily the one who had felled the victim and neither was the number of scalps taken the measure of one's prowess. Although the Sioux and Cree tended to put great stress on taking the scalp, the Blackfeet emphasized the number of guns or horses captured and it was also said 'you will never hear a Crow boast of his scalps'.

There was, nevertheless, a wide recognition that the scalp represented more than *just* a trophy from a conquered enemy. For example, the Piegan (Blackfeet) chief, *Saukamappee*, recounting a discussion between members of a successful war party relating to the significance of the scalps taken, reported that they had concluded that the souls of the Shoshone would now be their slaves 'in the other world'.

Scalping was by no means fatal (*right*), and sometimes an enemy was scalped alive and then sent back to his people as an act of defiance and as an incitement to retaliation.

Generally the skin was cut off the scalp if it was to be used for the embellishment of regalia. The two smaller scalps shown here (*below right*) belonged to the Blackfeet Indian, Crazy Crow. The larger one shown above them, decorated with porcupine quills and beads, is possibly of the Mandan tribe.

▲ Here the scalping has taken place (*bottom*). A victim removes his top hat to show his scalp wound (*middle right*) and scalps are shown as war trophies (*top*).

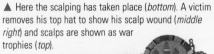

Arts and craft

Traditional Plains clothing was made of the dressed skin of buffalo, deer, antelope or bighorn. Dressing animal hides was an important craft and a woman's worth was estimated by her output.

The soles of moccasins, shaped containers known as *parfleches* and some horse equipment were made of a thin, stiff rawhide, whilst the uppers of moccasins, soft bags, shirts, leggings, dresses and robes were soft and pliable requiring a more elaborate preparation. The hide, cleaned of flesh using a special tool made of elk horn, was stretched on the ground or in a wooden frame and an oily mixture of brains, fat and liver rubbed into its surface. Left in the sun to dry, given several washings with warm water, it was then vigorously rubbed and stretched. The result was a fine, soft white hide which could be coloured by smoking over a fire or with earth paints, depending on its final use.

Skilled craftsmen, the Plains people used skin, stone, bone, horn, wood and feathers to produce ceremonial clothing – shirts, leggings, moccasins, headdresses and horse equipment – the decorative beauty and appeal of which is world renowned.

Men's shirts and women's dresses were made of two or more deer hides and whilst the style was the same throughout the Plains, decoration differed considerably between tribes. Children's costume was similar to their parents' and everyday clothing

▲ A Sioux woman tanning a hide which is stretched on a wooden frame. Hides needed to be carefully cleaned of fat and tissue: a typical chisel-like tool for this process is also shown here (*right*). This one has been made from part of a gun barrel but earlier examples were of bone. The other tool (*top right*) is made of elk horn and was used to remove the hair from the hide.

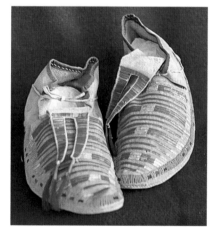

◄ Typical Plains Indian moccasins had soles of stiff, thin rawhide with uppers of soft buckskin. In the early days they were almost exclusively decorated with porcupine quillwork but later, after *circa* 1850, beads became increasingly popular. These moccasins, which are probably Sioux and date from 1880, show a combination of both types of embellishment.

resembled that used on ceremonial occasions, without the elaborate embellishments.

A typical man's ceremonial shirt had quilled or beaded bands across the shoulders and down the arms and hair (human or horse), ermine skin or buckskin fringes. Women's ceremonial dresses had long skirts with a cape-like top, decorated with quill or beadwork following the contours of the cape. Both sexes wore leggings, men's being long, tied to a belt and generally combined with a breechcloth, a broad strip of skin or cloth drawn up between the legs and under the belt. Women's leggings were short, extending from the ankle almost to the knee and supported by garters tied above the calf, with a wide panel of beadwork decorating the lower part.

The most popular style of bag, carried by the men, was long and slender. These 'pipe-bags', associated with the coveted pipes, were decorated in several ways, many being heavily beaded, with thin strips of rawhide wrapped with porcupine quills at the bottom and finished with long buckskin fringes. Also used for storage and referred to by the Sioux as 'a bag for every possible thing', they were made in pairs and decorated with porcupine quills and beads. Superbly ornamented, double saddle bags were also popular with the Central Plains tribes. The clever combination of function and artistic expression in these products, with their ingenious techniques and decorative appeal, is impressive.

► Rosa White Thunder, a Brulé Sioux photographed *circa* 1890. This fine young woman wears a superb dress made of trade cloth decorated with elk teeth. Note also her long dentalium shell earrings and belt studded with brass tacks. Her outfit reflects a style popular with the Sioux in the late nineteenth century.

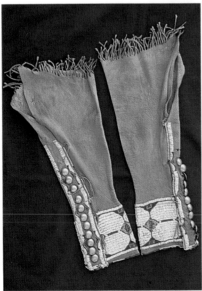

◄ Women's leggings made of deerskin and decorated with beadwork and German silver buttons which were collected from the Cheyenne in the region of the Canadian River in Oklahoma and date from *circa* 1890. The general cut and embellishment is typical of Plains women's leggings, although there were considerable variations in patterns within the beadwork and the sewing techniques used. Tied at the calf with garters, they had wide panels of bead-work on the lower part.

The destruction of Plains Indian culture

With the buffalo all but exterminated by 1884 much of the Plains Indians' culture had vanished. The destruction had begun more than a generation earlier with the first sizeable emigrations by white settlers in the early 1840s. The next two decades saw some two hundred thousand emigrants following the famous Oregon Trail which cut through the very heart of Plains Indian country. Not only did such large numbers of people destroy or frighten the game away, but the indigenous people were exposed to European diseases, such as whooping cough, cholera and smallpox, to which they had little or no immunity. To protect the settlers, many of the old fur trading forts, such as Laramie, Pierre and Union, were purchased by the government and turned into military posts.

Clashes were inevitable, the first major confrontation occurring near Fort Laramie in August 1854 between some thirty men commanded by Lieutenant John Grattan and a large number of Oglala Sioux warriors, including the young *Makhpiya-lúta*, 'Red Cloud' (who in years to come would emerge as an outstanding leader and diplomat). This tragic battle left all of Grattan's men dead and Grattan himself with twenty-four arrows in his body, one of which had gone completely through his head ... he could only be identified by his pocket watch.

So began the wars of suppression, with their brutal conflicts – Ash Hollow (1855), Sand Creek (1864), Washita (1868), the Sitting Bull wars of 1876, Custer's defeat (1876) and the death of Crazy Horse (1877) among them – underlining the immense differences between red and white cultures. The bitter confrontations ended in December 1890, on a small creek in South Dakota when the Miniconjou chief, Big Foot, and more than one hundred and forty of his band – men, women and children – died at the hands of the American cavalry. Spiritually, many more hearts were buried at Wounded Knee for it epitomized the final tragic end of the historic Plains Indian culture.

▲ Big Foot, chief of the Miniconjou Sioux, frozen in death at Wounded Knee. On 29 December 1890 three hundred Sioux surrendered to Major Whiteside of the Seventh Cavalry. As preparations were made to disarm the Sioux, a shot was fired and within seconds there was uncontrollable violence. Almost two hundred Sioux and twenty five soldiers died, amongst them Big Foot and most of the elder Miniconjou headmen.

NORTHEAST: LEAGUES AND GRAND SOCIETIES

Of birch bark and wampum

The Northeast cultural area is vast! It stretches from the northwestern shore of Lake Superior and then south to the confluence of the Cumberland and Ohio rivers. From here it stretches some one thousand miles (1,600km) east to the Atlantic coast. The northern border of this diverse area runs immediately south of the Lake of the Woods, in present-day western Ontario, extending to the North Carolina-Virginia coastal plain, a distance of about eleven hundred miles (1,770km) – in all, as with the Great Plains, encompassing an area of about one million square miles (about 2.6m sq km).

The people

The Northeast was occupied by almost forty tribes, several of which are well known, such as the Iroquois Confederacy which, after *circa* 1720, consisted of six separate tribes, the Mohawk, Oneida, Onondaga, Cayuga, Seneca and Tuscarora. Another tribe, the Mohicans (more correctly Mahican) of present-day northern Vermont, have been made famous by James Fenimore Cooper's *Last of the Mohicans* (first published in 1823). Today, together with their kinsmen, the Mohegan

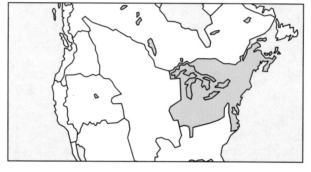

The Northeast cultural area extending from west of the Great Lakes eastwards to the Atlantic. These tribes were amongst the first to make contact with Whites.

and the Pequot of Connecticut, they are leading their tribes to a 'land of plenty' by running a highly successful casino (*see page 93*).

Two main linguistic stocks were spoken in the area, Iroquoian and Algonquian, although Siouan was also represented by tribes such as the Winnebago, who lived just west of Lake Michigan, and those in eastern Virginia, several of which were members of the powerful Powhatan Confederacy

◄ Land of the Mohican and Pennacook in present-day northern Vermont. This majestic country was the home of several Algonquian tribes who formed confederacies and warred against the Mohawk and other Iroquois tribes to the west.
In the middle distance are the maple trees which provided a rich source of sugar sap much coveted by these tribes as a nutritious food. This maple sugar was tapped from the trees every spring. It took several weeks to collect the required amount for winter use, providing an opportunity for joyous gatherings and co-ordinated group activities – a time to catch up on the previous year's gossip! A lengthy process of boiling, stirring, straining and pulverizing produced a fine form of highly nutritious granulated sugar, which could be used with fruits, vegetables, cereals and fish.

which held great sway in the vicinity of present-day Jamestown during the seventeenth century.

Because of the great variation in the lifestyle within this vast land it is usual to subdivide it into three geographic regions: Great Lakes-Riverine, Saint Lawrence Lowlands and Coastal, although it is often simply referred to as 'The Eastern Woodlands', or even just 'Woodlands'. Even with this tripartite division, there were some significant variations but broadly these smaller zones shared a common lifestyle. For example, in the Great Lakes-Riverine region, the predominant Central Algonquian tribes, such as the Chippewa (also called Ojibwa), Ottawa, Sauk and Fox, Miami, and Shawnee lived in birch bark wigwams, depended extensively on horticulture, gathered wild rice, travelled by birch bark canoe and fished in the countless lakes and streams in their territory. In contrast, whilst the basic lifestyle of the indigenous people of the Saint Lawrence Lowlands was similar, horticulture and fishing being also very important to their economy, tribes such as the Iroquois Confederacy traditionally lived in great longhouses which accommodated up to twenty families; they fortified their villages, used canoes of elm or spruce (since they lived below the birch line), and had a kinship system based on descent through the female line in contrast to the Great Lakes-Riverine region where it was through the male line.

Costume and face paint of the Fox Indians

The ceremonial costume of the Fox and adjacent tribes was often made of a complete animal hide, such as beaver, otter or young bear. This costume was a highly coveted garment, generally beyond the command of any but a very privileged few. Often the entire skin, including head, tail, feet and even the claws, was preserved and richly garnished with coloured cloth, beads, birds' feathers and down.

Shown here is *Nesouaquoit* or 'The Bear in the Forks of a Tree', who was a distinguished chief of the Fox tribe and whose portrait was painted by the artist Charles Bird King when *Nesouaquoit* was in Washington during the winter of 1837. His poncho is of bearskin, the eyes of the animal worked in red cloth and beads, the ears intact and with a symbolic representation of the bear's paws on the shoulders. Whole animal skins were used to signify the animal's spirit powers, the prowess of the bear, in this case, being transferred to the wearer.

This portrait also shows *Nesouaquoit* wearing a superb turban embellished with beads and surmounted by a brooch made of

◀ Portrait by Charles Bird King of *Nesouaquoit* or 'The Bear in the Forks of a Tree', a distinguished chief of the Fox tribe, who is wearing ceremonial costume and face paint.

horse and porcupine guard hair. Around his neck is a 'peace medal' bearing a representation of the President of the United States. Such medals were given as gifts to chiefs by government officials, in recognition of their high status.

His body paint, showing bands of red on both arms and face, possibly refers to deeds accomplished in battle, each stripe symbolizing a

coup. Sauk and Fox warriors often wore magnificent necklaces made of grizzly bear claws as a sign of their status (as shown in the portrait of *Keokuk, see page 26*).

This painting, amongst the first produced by the artist Charles Bird King, has been regarded as his masterpiece and is one of the most remarkable examples of Indian portraiture in existence.

Population distribution of the tribes throughout the area was similar to that of the Great Plains (*see Chapter 1*). In 1760 the Chippewa numbered about twenty-five thousand, the Iroquois some sixteen thousand, while many of the tribes in the Powhatan Confederacy seldom exceeded one thousand and the Chesapeake, Powhatan and Appomattoc only a few hundred. These figures are generally estimates as contact with Whites was limited and many tribes were nearly destroyed by European diseases. For example, the Micmac – an Algonquian-speaking tribe who lived in the Atlantic Provinces of Canada – numbered about four thousand five hundred at the time of the first European contact by the Venetian explorer, John Cabot, in 1497. They were then constantly visited by explorers and vessels from France and England and acted as middlemen between the Europeans and the Indians farther west and south. At that time, the Micmac had few diseases – rheumatism, gout, fevers were unknown – the French describing them as a handsome, vigorous and healthy people. However, with the introduction of pleurisy, quinsy, dysentery and smallpox, as well as alcoholism and warfare, the population progressively declined and in 1650 it was only about two thousand. The Micmac became increasing involved in the fur trade and dependent upon European trade goods, particularly metal knives, axes and kettles. The English, who gained

◀ *Keokuk*, chief of the Sauk and Fox. *Keokuk* was not a chief by birth but rose to prominence through marked ability, great oratory and force of character. With great skill in debate with both Sioux and government officials he established the claim of the Sauk and Fox to the territory which is now Iowa. This photograph was taken from a daguerreotype about 1847, one year before *Keokuk* died. Note the fine bear claw necklace and turban – distinctive costume of tribes in the region of Iowa and Missouri.

▶ The Huron chief, Matthew Mudeater, photographed in Washington in 1875. The Huron were a powerful and highly organized confederation of four tribes, about twenty thousand strong, who occupied a territory referred to as Huronia, an area around Lake Simcoe and south and east of Georgian Bay, Ontario. By the late nineteenth century the tribe had been reduced – by smallpox and war with the Iroquois – to less than one thousand. The spirit of a proud race is written in the features of this chief, but traditional costume has completely gone.

Micmac territory from the French in 1713, confined them to reservations, so destroying the traditional hunting and fishing economy.

The Micmac were and still are a resilient people, rapidly adapting to the changes they faced. The men began making wooden craft items and baskets, while the women, drawing on their traditional skills and knowledge, produced greatly prized souvenirs of birch bark which were lavishly embellished with quillwork and natural or dyed split spruce root.

The changing fortunes of the Micmac under the impact of Europeans, was a pattern which would be replicated throughout the Northeastern culture area with even more dire consequences. The Huron population was decimated by a smallpox epidemic in the winter of 1639, declining further due to warfare with the Iroquois caused by fur trade interests. A virtual war of extermination led to the adoption of many Huron by the Iroquois, others fled west, whilst a few found refuge at Lorette near Quebec City. By the early 1900s, it is estimated that less than one thousand Huron remained and Huronia, their ancient homeland, was abandoned.

The Lorette Huron and the Coastal Zone Micmac further north and east, turned their craft skills to good advantage, producing exquisitely embroidered objects from moosehair (taken from the bell or dewlap) and selling them as souvenirs, providing an important source of income.

Warfare and weapons

Inter-tribal warfare pivoted on a web of issues, the desire for new territory, better hunting grounds, for women and children, to prove a warrior's prowess or simply for revenge; and preparation for war was a serious matter. Thus, prior to moving against the enemy, warriors of the Powhatan Confederacy of seventeenth century Virginia, engaged in 'mimic' warfare – war games – in order to be prepared and to be successful.

To ensure victory, the mode of warfare was one of surprise and sometimes even treachery. The great chief *Powhatan* had no hesitation in employing both methods when in 1608 he set out to destroy a neighbouring tribe, the Piankatank, who would not conform to his regime. First, he sent a few of his men to lodge with the Piankatank on the pretence of organizing a hunt. When the village was asleep, the Powhatan warriors signalled to the rest of the war party, who were hidden in the surrounding forest. They stormed the village and massacred the occupants. The women and children who survived were presented to *Powhatan* by the exalted victors, whilst the scalps of the men who had been killed were taken to the town of Werowocomoco, near present-day Jamestown, Virginia. There they were hung on a line and pointed out to visiting English traders with a view to cowering them by such a ghastly spectacle.

In comparison to the Powhatans, Chippewa warfare was virtually a game and large-scale massacres were rare. There were, however, major conflicts in the nineteenth century when the Chippewa, who for years had been in contact with traders and hence had guns, waged war on the Sioux who, armed only with the bow, were driven west and out of their traditional homelands of Wisconsin and eastern Minnesota. Many scalp dances and songs were sung around the camp-fires at this time by the victorious Chippewa:

gonige' tagina'	I wonder
agadendamodog'	if she is humiliated
Oma'mikwe'	the Sioux woman
gikic'kigwejug'	that I cut off her head

(Chippewa Scalp Song, sung by *Odjibwe*)

The tomahawk

The term 'tomahawk' was originally applied to a group of weapons commonly used by the Algonquian tribes of the eastern United States. Early writers mention the word from this region with slight variations as *tomahack* or *tommahick*, whilst the Mahican (Mohican) called their weapons, *tumnahecan*.

The early tomahawk was made of wood with a long handle and a round head made of a ball of solid wood which was, as one writer said, 'heavy enough … to knock men's brains out'. Sometimes a flint or bone point was inserted into the ball, making it a very dangerous weapon at close quarters.

Often decorated with feathers and paint, the entire tomahawk was painted red, when council was called to deliberate war. It was then placed on the ground by the chief and if the council decreed that a war party should be raised, the leader of the young warriors picked up the tomahawk, dancing and singing the war songs. The message was then delivered to surrounding friendly tribes, a 'belt of wampum' being sent to commemorate the decision, and a combined war party was raised.

At an early period, metal axes were traded to the eastern tribes and later, certainly by the late 1700s, the pipe tomahawk was introduced. These were described by the English as 'smoak tomahawks' as they were a combination of weapon and pipe. Early styles, such as that carried by *Ki-on-twog-ky* or 'Cornplanter' a Seneca (Iroquois Confederacy) chief in 1796 were, as shown here, a combination of a trade metal spiked weapon and clay pipe bowl. Later

metal ones moulded both the blade and bowl into one. These weapons were handled with great dexterity and it seems they were frequently *thrown* at the enemy with such accuracy that they seldom failed, as one early observer reported, to 'strike it into the skull or back of those they pursue'.

Longhouses and wigwams

The traditional dwelling of most tribes of the Saint Lawrence Lowlands was a basic framework of upright posts enclosing a rectangular floor area and accommodating one family. The traditional Iroquois home was similar but considerably larger and, since the tribe lived below the birch line, was covered with large sheets of bark – generally from the elm tree. These dwellings could be up to sixty-five feet (20m) in length and twenty feet (6m) high and were known as *ganonh'sees*, the 'longhouse'. There was a door at each end with a passageway running down the centre on each side of which were small platformed rooms occupied by separate families. Pairs of families were served by small fires set at intervals along the length of the *ganonh'sees*, the smoke escaping through holes in the roof. Towards the end of the eighteenth century, there was a gradual shift towards single family dwellings and the longhouse became a council house for the whole community. Even today the longhouse, although a modern building, is considered a key symbol of tribal unity.

More widely distributed was the wigwam, a term adopted from the Abnaki and Micmac which in their Eastern Algonquian dialect means 'dwelling' and can, in fact, refer to both arbour- or conically-shaped dwellings which were covered with bark and or mats. A well-constructed wigwam – be it

The wigwam

The term 'wigwam' derives from the Abnaki (Eastern Algonquian) language meaning 'dwelling'. The early colonists adopted the word to describe any form of Indian dwelling, be it arbour- or conically-shaped. In fact, great variations occurred in terminology from one Algonquian tribe to the next, so the Lenape (Delaware) use *wikwam* and the Chippewa, *wigiwami*. To the west and north, in the Great Lakes-Riverine zone, the Chippewa and adjacent tribes, such as the Menominee and Winnebago, used domed wigwams. The general mode of erection was the same from Canada to North Carolina and variations occurred depending upon the plant materials available. Tribes of the Powhatan Confederacy, for example, who occupied much of Virginia in the early sixteenth century, used grass matting so tightly woven that it was waterproof (*below left*).

The domed wigwam consisted of a circular or rectangular foundation of long flexible poles which were pushed into the ground and then bent over to produce a number of arches. Horizontal saplings were then tied to the arch poles, creating a net-like frame. The frame was then covered with large mats woven from cattail (*Typha latifolia*), leaving a small aperture at the top as a smoke hole. Next, sheets of birch bark up to six feet long and three feet wide (approximately 2m x 1m) were laid over the mats, overlapping as one would shingle a roof; these in turn were tied in place with basswood fibres. Two birch bark layers were usual for summer wigwams, three or more for winter use. A small fire was provided by a number of logs radiating from the hearth which were pushed inward as they burnt, the wood carefully selected to ensure a minimum of smoke. A firm platform extending part of the way around the interior served both as seating and beds.

Frances Densmore, the ethnologist who studied the Chippewa for over twenty years, was greatly impressed with the comfort, warmth and beauty of their wigwams.

▲ Exterior of a reconstructed Powhatan wigwam. The village site which dates back to about 1650 is near present-day Richmond, Virginia.

▲ Interior of the wigwam. Note the large fireplace, beds covered with skins and wooden mortars in which maize and beans were pounded.

◀ A typical dwelling of birch bark and willow poles lashed together with spruce roots and ash splints. This house was erected by Joseph and Newell Thomas, two Passamaquoddy craftsmen, at the request of the Bureau of American Ethnology.

Chippewa or Powhatan – was a very practical and comfortable dwelling, well adapted to its environment whatever the weather. Frances Densmore, a close observer of the Chippewa in the early twentieth century, was greatly impressed with the beauty and warmth of the winter wigwam ... 'where the winter evenings were social and pleasant ... the fire burned brightly ... a favourite pastime was making birch-bark transparencies ... the winter was the time for story-telling ... and ... one old woman used to act out her stories, running around the fire and acting while she talked'.

The Woodland village was always carefully sited ensuring good sources of wood, water and protection from enemies. Some villages were fortified, particularly those of the early Virginian Algonquians and Iroquoians in the vicinity of Chesapeake Bay. Typical was the town of Pomeiooc visited by the Englishman, John White, in the late 1580s. All were close to rivers, streams or lakes which could be rapidly traversed by canoe.

The birch bark canoe

The Northeastern cultural area was heavily forested, dotted with lakes and laced with rivers and streams, in short ideal for travel by water. Tribes such as the Chippewa, Passamaquoddy, Maliseet and Menominee were skilled in the production of birch bark canoes, but the Chippewa were recognized as both expert builders and canoemen. Sizes of craft varied considerably but those designed to carry a family were some sixteen feet (5m) in length and three feet (lm) wide at the middle. Building a canoe was a joint effort of both men and women, supervised by a person skilled in the craft. All the materials used came from trees: the framework and the lining were of cedar, the cords used to bind the frame were of split spruce root and the seal for the seams was made from spruce gum, which was usually boiled to thicken it and then mixed with powdered charcoal which gave an ornamental appearance to the caulking. Most importantly, the bark which was to be used for the covering was carefully selected, ensuring that it was of the right thickness – perhaps up to nine separate layers. It was thoroughly soaked to make it pliable, then sections were laid on the ground and weighted down with a narrow flat frame which defined the approximate length as well as the width of the canoe. The bark was then eased upwards using several short poles driven into the ground at a slight angle and the gunwales put into place. The women now sewed the bark into place using split, wet spruce root, always ensuring that the overlapping edges of the bark were towards the end of the canoe to give a streamlined flow of water around the contours. The ribbed cross pieces, of varying widths, and the lining of thin strips of cedar, were then put in place and all the seams caulked with blackened spruce gum. The canoe was propelled using paddles made of cedar or birch wood. Generally the woman would travel in the stern and the man in the prow. As one observer, George Catlin, reported on the Chippewa canoe, they are 'so ingeniously shaped and sewed together ... that they ... ride upon the water, as light as cork'.

▲ A fine sixteen foot (5m) birch bark canoe made by Maranda, a Rapid Lake Algonquin. He was the last of the master birch bark canoe makers who died in 1987. His canoes were characterized by a particularly elegant gunwale line.

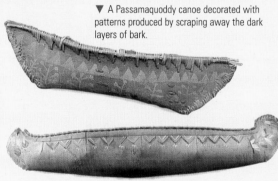

▼ A Passamaquoddy canoe decorated with patterns produced by scraping away the dark layers of bark.

▲ A fine model birch bark canoe decorated with coloured procupine quills.

World view and religious concepts

A well-defined 'World View' in the Northeastern culture area, broadly shared by both the Iroquoian and Algonquian speakers, was underlined by the principles advocated in the foundation of the League of the Iroquois around 1570. Emphasis was put on creating a society where health, happiness, righteousness, justice, power and individual strength of character were paramount. There was also recognition that man was to be considered as only a part of the complex web of the natural world, which itself could neither be owned nor unfairly exploited and where anything taken was to be repaid. This pattern of behaviour was transmitted orally from one generation to the next by carefully selected tribal historians.

An annual council was called by the centrally placed Onondagas, who were also the 'keepers of the wampum belts' (which documented tribal history using symbolic motifs worked in beads). It was then that the constitution of the League was rehearsed and any differences resolved. It has been suggested that the League of the Iroquois, its democratic principles, laws and regulations were an inspiration to the main writers of the American Constitution, who were familiar with its structure.

There was a recognition that life was everywhere – both visible and invisible, beneath the ground and under the waters. These powers

The Chippewa herbalist

The Chippewa gave particular priority to health. Nearly all their homes had an assortment of herbs and roots hanging on the walls, ceilings and over the fire – each one a cure for some malady. These ranged from those with actual medicinal effect, such as laxatives, to herbs which were said to have magical properties, such as the root of milkwort (*Polygala senega L.*), and were carried on the person for safety on a journey. More than one hundred, and forty plants were known to the Chippewa of Minnesota and Wisconsin, a number of which, after scientific analysis, have been found to have therapeutic properties.

This interest and knowledge goes back centuries in Chippewa culture and was a major concern of the *Midewiwin* Society who put great emphasis on prolonging life by 'right living'. The teachings of the Society were inscribed on birch bark rolls, the significance of the pictographs being taught to the initiates. Members carried special bags, often made of the complete skin of an animal, such as an otter or beaver, and containing charms and a variety of medicinal herbs, which the owner had been taught to use. The charms were symbolic of the spirit forces, the herbs evoking the curative powers.

Bear power was frequently evoked by the *Midewiwin* doctors and bear claws decorated with beads, brass tacks and ribbons were used to ward off evil spirits.

The Chippewa Indians' interest in healing has found expression today in a herbal medicine used to treat cancer. Named *Essiac* one of its most important ingredients is 'sheep's sorrel'. The formula was obtained in the 1920s from a Chippewa herbalist by Dr. Charles A. Brusch of Massachusetts who was the personal physician of the late John F. Kennedy and who reported after ten years research that '*Essiac* is a cure for cancer, period'.

▲ A Chippewa *Jes'sakkid* 'medicine man' removing disease from a patient by sucking through a bone tube. Medicine men were believed to have received their powers from the *Animiki* or 'Thunder God'.

▲ A *Midewiwin* (Chippewa) grizzly bear claw fetish.

were associated with the *Manitou* of the Algonquians and *Orenda* of the Iroquois and were often evoked by offerings on high medicine poles above the dwelling. Ancestors were to be revered since they were strong, dignified, healthy, generous, just and brave. Their behaviour should be an inspirational guide to their descendants, mythology relating to origins, the Sun, Moon, Earth, Sky Woman, Thunderbirds, Monsters and other supernatural beings, making reference to the power and influence of the ancestors. Men are or, at least, should be equal, no one putting himself above others. However, men with unusual abilities and who followed the traditional patterns of generosity, fairness and courage should be allowed to lead.

The Woodland tribes also made a distinction between the religious concepts of Indians and non-Indians. Indians always had supernatural helpers who could bring them special gifts or messages – the Micmac said some individuals possessed *keskamizit*, or 'Indian luck' enabling them to find, do, or make things with great reliability or speed.

These concepts were firmly embedded in the religious teachings of the Chippewa *Midewiwin*, or Grand Medicine Society, emphasis being put on ethical conduct and the interpretation of dreams and visions which were viewed as messages from the supernatural powers. Only those fulfilling these criteria could qualify to become great healers.

◄ An Iroquois beaded bag, possibly Mohawk, and dating from *circa* 1870. Such bags, based on traditional styles of beadwork, became particularly popular with the arrival of tourists to Iroquois country after *circa* 1860. The use of beads in two shades of one colour is typical of the beadwork done at this period. The birds worked on the flap and body of the bag are, however, far less common, motifs generally consisting of flowers and plants.

► An Iroquois corn husk doll wearing a False Face mask. This model illustrates two important facets of Iroquoian society: the method of making corn husk dolls which were originally used in certain medicine rites and the importance of masks to the Iroquois. Masks were worn by the members of various societies in several ceremonies, some of which were held for the purpose of exorcising evil spirits and driving away diseases.

Subsistence

A vast abundance of food was available to the Woodland tribes: wild fruits, such as blueberries, raspberries, gooseberries, grapes and cherries; nuts of various kinds, such as hazel, beech, hickory and butter, and wild potatoes and onions, the latter being a particular favourite. All these, together with the wild rice, *Zizania aquatica*, were the main components of the vegetable diet particularly of the Chippewa and Menominee tribes of the Western Great Lakes region. Throughout a large area the sap was tapped from the maple trees and collected every spring, providing an opportunity for joyous gatherings and co-ordinated group activities.

The Iroquois, Huron and other tribes of the Saint Lawrence Lowlands, also made great use of the natural resources available to them, indeed it has been established that they collected more than thirty wild fruits, eleven varieties of nuts, twelve types of edible roots and nearly forty varieties of bark, leaf and stem products, as well as six fungi. Added to this were 'the three sisters' – maize, squashes, and beans – which were regarded as sacred gifts from the Creator. Meat was a relatively small part of the diet of both Iroquois and Huron, although the region teamed with game – caribou, wapiti (elk), deer and moose. Hunting, however, was essential to provide hides for clothing, moccasins and various accoutrements.

SOUTHEAST: MONARCHS AND RUNAWAYS

Of mounds and Mound-Builders

Although boundaries changed with time, progressively reducing its size, the historic cultural area of the Southeast (*circa* 1700 onwards), was bounded by the Mississippi River to the west, the Atlantic Ocean to the east and south to the Gulf of Mexico. Its northern boundary extended into present-day Kentucky and Virginia. The indigenous culture of this vast region of more than one million square miles (2.6m sq km), has been likened to a great shattered bowl, the innumerable pieces of which present historians, archaeologists and anthropologists alike, with an almost impossible task when they attempt to recreate the original.

Nevertheless, several discernable patterns and themes have emerged which document an area occupied by man thousands of years before the Christian era and which, at certain periods, displayed definite influences from both Mexico and South America and, in early years, extended well beyond the historic boundaries.

The region was, and still is, dotted with thousands of mounds, some small, others enormous, man-made hills and mostly used for burial purposes. Others depict great, sprawling effigies of men, beasts or birds, such as the Serpent

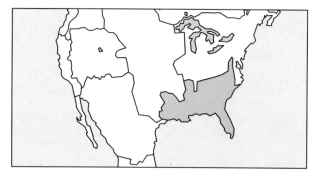

Most of the Southeast cultural area falls within the broad coastal plain which borders the Atlantic and the Gulf of Mexico, taking in all of present-day Florida.

Mound in Ohio, which is more than a quarter-mile (0.4km) in length and without doubt the world's largest serpent effigy. These Mound-Builders flourished for more than three thousand years but by about AD600 the so-called Adena-Hopewell culture was largely in decline to be replaced by a major new culture centred on the fertile lands of the Mississippi Valley; with confederations of tribes and a 'war game' complex … warfare for its own sake.

◄ The Florida Everglades, home of the Seminole Indians. The region is often described as a 'river of grass' and teems with wildlife: otters, alligators, many wading birds and the mysterious manatee, which resemble a whale with a prehensile lip and a broad, flattened tail.

Ribbonwork of the Seminole

The Seminole, principally the Mikasuki group, acquired hand-cranked sewing machines from white traders in the late 1800s, together with a variety of calicos, coloured cloth and ribbons. The new device and materials led to the development of cut and sewn patchwork which first appeared as relatively simple bands or strips of contrasting colours on both men's and women's costume, as shown in this early photograph of the Seminole woman, Mrs. John Tiger. Later, the stitched decorations became more elaborate and emerged as a distinctive feature of Seminole costume.

The full beauty of this work – which historic photographs fail to capture – is illustrated by this bag (*right*) collected from the Seminole near the Big Cypress Reservation in the Florida Everglades. The designs shown here are traditional and of a type which have been used for many years in this region, whilst those from other reservations, such as Brighton near Lake Okeechobee to the north, sometimes differed. Since about 1940 Seminole women

◀ Mrs. John Tiger, photographed in the Big Cypress Reservation about 1932. She wears typical Seminole woman's costume for the period. Her husband, John Tiger, died at about this time and she retreated into the depths of the Everglades, remaining there for some time in mourning.

▼ A Seminole bag decorated with ribbonwork and with a base of woven cane and reeds. This type of patchwork decoration began on a small scale in about 1890 and became increasingly elaborate with the passage of time. Today it continues to be a popular form of decoration.

have tended to alternate rows of ribbon trims with bands of patchwork. On the Big Cypress Reservation, six or more bands of small designs were used, whilst on the Brighton Reservation just one wide band was more popular. Because designs were often admired, they were copied and hence widely used.

The Mississippian culture

This so-called Mississippian culture, was strongly influenced by those of Mexico, the great mounds now becoming bases for temples, hence the description Temple Mound period. Maize, beans, chilli and squash were now grown in abundance and elaborate ceremonials, several of which were associated with death and human sacrifice, were held annually. These clearly had a Mexican inspiration, possibly under the stimulus of Mexican traders who introduced ideas, as well as goods, from a distant exotic land.

These Southeastern tribes obtained raw materials via an ancient and complex trade network – Caribbean conch shells, Appalachian mica, Great Lakes copper, Minnesota pipestone and even silver from Canada – and turned them into engraved shell gorgets, a collar-like throat armour; the mica sheets into elaborate silhouettes, and copper into axes, fish hooks and thin sheets for use as ceremonial plaques; pipes were elaborately carved depicting birds and mammals. All reflected a society which contained talented specialists who had both time and energy to turn to the arts, so documenting for posterity, a culture rich in pageantry and ceremonial, which was unparalleled anywhere in Native North America.

The zenith of the Mississippian culture is exemplified by the ancient city of Cahokia which

◄ The zenith of early Mississippian culture is illustrated by the Cahokia mound just west of present-day St. Louis, Missouri. Flourishing about AD1200, the mound was the focus of a city which housed an estimated 30,000 inhabitants. The culture reflected influence from ancient Mexico.

◄ *Sequoya*, the Cherokee mixed-blood who devised a syllabary and so enabled his people to become literate – even publishing their own newspaper. *Sequoya* died in Mexico in 1843.

flourished about AD1200 and was located just west of present-day St. Louis, Missouri. Here, a huge mound some one hundred feet (30.5m) high and extending over sixteen acres (6.5ha) (surpassing the Great Pyramid of Egypt), was the focus of a city which housed an estimated 30,000 inhabitants. The mound was surmounted by a thatched temple in which burned a sacred fire. Ceremonials carried out in the temple were dedicated to sun worship, several of which included human sacrifice. This pattern, although on a smaller scale, was replicated throughout the Southeast extending from present-day Oklahoma, south to Florida. The culture

flourished for more than five hundred years – until about AD1200 – then, for reasons not fully understood, faded into oblivion, although remnants of the culture were observed by the French in the late 1600s, amongst the Natchez of Mississippi.

The final death knell of the great Mississippian culture occurred when the power of the Natchez was destroyed by wars with the French in the 1730s, who then sold the survivors into slavery. So ended the most highly developed culture achieved by any Indian group north of Mexico. Many historic tribes simply disappeared, the great Creek Confederacy emerging from the chiefdoms.

▲ These rare moccasins, dating from before 1850, are embellished with tiny seed beads combined with gold-plated beads. They are typical of the moccains from this region, and are made of smoked buckskin with soft soles and the ankle flaps bound with silk ribbon.

The Five Civilized Tribes

The progressive demise of the Mississippian culture, not only caused the indigenous inhabitants to relocate and reorganize but enabled new groups to move in from the North and Northeast. By the late seventeenth century, the heart of the Southeast was occupied by two major linguistic groups, Muskogean and Iroquoian. The former was represented by such tribes as Choctaws, Creeks and Chickasaws whose domain extended across much of present-day Mississippi, Georgia and Alabama, whilst in the north in present-day Tennessee and North Carolina, were the Iroquoian-speaking Cherokee. South in present-day Florida, still lived the Timucua and Calusa tribes with whom Europeans had first made contact in the early sixteenth century. Later, in the 1580s, the lifestyle of the Timucua was documented by the French artist, Jacques Le Moyne, who recorded the hunting, habitations, customs, arts and mode of travel of these people, in great detail.

The closing years of the seventeenth century, saw the Southeastern tribes encircled by Europeans – the French to the west, Spanish on the south and English to the north – each attempting to gain Indian allies, vital links in the flourishing and lucrative fur trade. It was, however, the English with their rapidly developing industries who could offer the best bargains and soon British traders were living amongst the Creek, Cherokee and Chickasaw. The French and Indian War (1755–63) and subsequent treaty of 1763 eliminated France from the New World and Spanish influence no longer extended farther east than the Mississippi: the lands from the Hudson Bay to the Gulf of Mexico, as well as Florida, came under British rule. The occupation lasted for twelve years before the British were ousted by the thirteen American colonies during the War of Independence. By the 1820s the tribes, which included a high proportion of mixed-bloods with names such as Ross, McIntosh and Weatherford, had learnt that a policy of negotiation and re-organization was preferable to confrontation. The increasing influx of Whites led to a demand for more land and over a period of nearly a decade (1832–1839), the tribes – which later included the Seminole – were progressively moved to Indian Territory (present-day Oklahoma). There was much bitterness and resistance but it was to no avail, as one Creek woman lamented:

> *I have no more land*
> *I am driven away from home*
> *Driven up the red waters*
> *Let us all go*
> *Let us all die together*

This sentiment would be echoed down the years by many members of the Five Civilized Tribes.

▲ The Cherokee, *Ayyuini*, better known as 'Swimmer'. This highly esteemed medicine man recorded the sacred curing formulas of his tribe using the syllabary invented by *Sequoya* (*see opposite*).

The Trail of Tears

The Treaty of Echota signed in 1835 by the Cherokee, ceded to the United States for five million dollars, the whole of remaining Cherokee lands east of the Mississippi River. As part of the agreement, new lands in Indian Territory (now Oklahoma) were placed at the disposal of the Cherokee for settlement. Facing the inevitable, some – such as the chief, Tahchee – embraced the chance of a lifestyle free of white influence. The tribe, however, became divided into two factions, one of which bitterly opposed the move and it became clear to the United States

Government that the removal could only be accomplished by force. In 1838, General Winfield Scott was given the task of the removal, and precipitated a human tragedy hardly surpassed in American history. By persuasion, by bribery, by fraud and above all by brutal force, thousands of Cherokee were uprooted from their ancient homelands and moved to a far and unfriendly land. In particular the forced migration of the Cherokee in the winter of 1838–39 is remembered as the 'Trail of Tears' for an estimated 4,000 died on route, including three hundred who died in a steamboat disaster.

▲ Cherokee chief, Tahchee

'dugout' canoe to negotiate the swamplands. Whilst there were no formal schools, girls learnt to sew, do traditional craftwork, cook and tend the children and boys accompanied their fathers and uncles on hunting and fishing trips. Community spirit and hospitality were a vital ingredient of Seminole life with much visiting between camps.

From their earliest times in Florida, the Seminole had offered both freedom and sanctuary to the black slaves escaping from the plantations of Alabama and Georgia which led to frequent border clashes with the white slave-owners. A long series of bitter disputes aggravated by the Indian Removal Act of 1830, led to the so-called Seminole Wars and a progressive removal of Seminoles to Oklahoma, extending from 1817 to 1855. Patriots, such as

The Seminole

The Creek tribe consists of two main groups, the Upper and Lower Creeks and even as early as 1703, several families from the Lower Creek towns of Georgia had migrated into what is now the state of Florida, occupying land previously owned by the Timucua, who had largely disappeared due to war and the ravages of European disease. They absorbed the few remaining Timucua and Calusa Indians and this combined group became the Seminole (from the Creek word *sim-a-no'le*, meaning a runaway, undomesticated, wild).

They retreated to the Everglades of Florida and by the 1850s had adapted well to the semi-tropical climate, creating small communities of several camps, referred to as *hammocks*. Traditional Creek houses, known as *chickees*, were open-sided and thatched with palmetto fronds. A platform of split logs raised them from the ground, giving protection from mud, damp and insects. The camps had a central cookhouse where communal meals were eaten. There was an abundance of plant and animal life and the Seminole learnt to become adept hunters of alligators and turtles using an elegant

▲ Mikasuki Seminole poling dugout canoes through the Florida Everglades. Both men and women are wearing highly decorated ribbonwork garments so typical of the tribe by the late nineteenth century. (*See Ribbonwork of the Seminole, page 33*).

Osceola, refused to move but, under a flag of truce, he was seized and subsequently died a prisoner at Fort Moultrie in South Carolina in 1838. Others, such as Billy Bowlegs, were more successful. Following a battle at Lake Okeechobee in 1855, he won the right for some Seminoles to remain in the Everglades, descendants of whom are still there.

Halpatter-Micco or Billy Bowlegs

This Seminole chief was amongst the very last leaders of his tribe to hold out against white intrusion. *Halpatter-Micco* was one of the principal leaders in the so-called Third Seminole War which broke out in 1855 and took place near Lake Okeechobee in the depths of the Florida Everglades. The protest led to an agreement that some of the remaining Seminole could continue to occupy their traditional homelands and it is from this independent group that many of the present-day Seminole are descended. This portrait by Charles Bird King is probably based on an early daguerreotype taken in New Orleans in 1858. It shows the colourful Seminole costume of the period – an engraved silver headband surmounted by coloured ostrich feathers (obtained in trade from Whites), hand-woven sashes decorated with beadwork and the popular crescent-shaped metal gorget (throat armour) which, traditionally at least, was a sign of military rank.

In personal appearance *Halpatter-Micco* was considered a good looking man. He had a high, broad forehead and dark brown eyes. He was of above average height and well-built. The name 'Bowlegs' had no reference to any physical peculiarity, but was simply a family nickname. In 1858 Billy Bowlegs left his native Florida, which he had fought so hard to protect, and with one hundred and thirteen followers, including his two wives and six children, moved to Indian Territory where he had been given land. He died there about 1865.

◀ *Osceola*, or 'Black drink crier', a chief and principal leader in the early years of the Seminole Wars of 1835–42. He died, probably of malaria, in January 1838. He is now described as a hero to today's Florida Seminoles and a number of families perpetuate his name.

SOUTHWEST: LAND OF ANCIENTS AND NEWCOMERS

Of deserts and canyons

The Southwest culture area extended from the southern borders of Utah and Colorado, encompassed the whole of Arizona and New Mexico, stretching south across the Mexican border to include the island of San Esteban and east across to Sonora, home of such tribes as the Seri, Yaqui, Mayo and Tahue. Much of the region is semi-arid or arid but it is a land of stark contrast and impressive scenery. To the north, at elevations five thousand feet (1,600m) or more, there are immense flat-topped tablelands with steep edges known as mesas, a number carved by the elements into fantastical shapes, such as those in Monument Valley which resemble, at a distance, gigantic cathedrals. To the west is the Grand Canyon carved more than a mile (1.6km) deep by the rushing waters of the Colorado River. The southern half of the area consists of great areas of level, dry and sometimes very hot desert, broken in places by tortuous mountain ranges, intermittent streams, scattered juniper trees and clumps of piñon and cactus. Annual rainfall varies throughout this vast land but seldom exceeds twenty inches (51cm) – then usually in a violent deluge momentarily flooding the dry terrain, only to disappear within less than an hour.

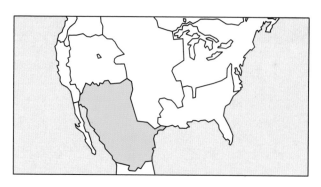

The Southwest cultural area extends from Utah and Colorado, south into Mexico. A land of desert, canyons and mesas, it was ancient territory for almost sixty tribes, including the largest in North America – the Navajo.

▲ Amongst the best of the artistic achievements of the ancient settlers of the Southwest region was pottery. Illustrated here is a Hohokam bowl dating from *circa* AD1200. Graceful and with a deep bell shape, it features curvilinear designs in its scrolls and wavy hatching.

The Desert and Hohokam peoples

This land of contrasts, fostered a diversity of lifestyles. First was the Archaic Desert Tradition culture which depended upon the gathering of roots, seeds, cactus fruits and the trapping of small game. Living in caves and brush shelters and practising basketry, the Desert culture flourished for several thousand years BC. Gradual changes came about due to the introduction of pottery, maize and later beans and squash from Mexico – the beginnings of horticulture. Thus, by about 200BC, the prehistoric Hohokam, a group strongly committed to farming, had emerged.

They occupied a vast, torrid plain broken by volcanic hills and rocky outcrops and extending across present-day southern Arizona and into Mexico. The limited supply of wild fruits and roots in their terrain turned the Hohokam into very efficient masters of irrigation; they tapped the Gila River, so watering their cornfields with an elaborate network of canals and ditches. Numerous villages and small towns emerged with the Hohokam culture, a pattern quite alien to the earlier Desert Tradition. Lasting until about AD1400 it absorbed other settled farming tribes from the north and west. Towards the end of this time they built enormous dwellings of adobe (sun-dried bricks), examples of which can still be seen at Casa Grande near present-day Phoenix, Arizona. The descendants of the Hohokam became the Pima and Papago of historic times, while other remnants are the Seri of the arid coast of Sonora but whose contemporary culture was much influenced by neighbouring tribes such as the Pima, Papago and Yaqui.

◀ Descendants of the ancient peoples of Arizona and New Mexico were such tribes as the Seri, who live in Sonora, Mexico. This Seri man, bow and arrow in hand, stands before his brush shelter of a type which probably dates back thousands of years.

▶ The Southwest is a land of stark contrast and impressive scenery but much, as shown here on the Navajo Reservation in Arizona, consists of a level and dry desert broken by mountain ranges and scattered with clumps of cactus and piñon.

◄ This fine Seri girl of the Sonora desert, although photographed in the late nineteenth century, lived a lifestyle similar to that of the ancient inhabitants of Arizona and New Mexico, such as the Mogollon and Hohokam peoples – cultures which had died out in that region by *circa* AD1200.

The Anasazi

To the north of this region another culture developed – that of the Anasazi, which flowered from about AD900 to 1300. Towards the end of this period the Anasazi began to build dwellings above ground using stone and producing remarkable habitations up to five storeys high and often set into cliffs. This became the period of 'cliff dwellers', each small town – called a Pueblo by the Spanish – consisting of terraced apartment houses, each self-contained, and having a population of up to eight thousand. Several happenings put an end to the Anasazi culture, not least changing climatic conditions and conflicts with prowling, aggressive nomads – Athapascans – who migrated into the region from the far north.

The River and Desert Pueblos

One by one, the great villages were deserted, the inhabitants moving to more fertile and safer regions. One group drifted to the region of the Rio Grande, others west to the deserts of Arizona, ultimately to be classified by anthropologists as River and Desert Pueblos. Of the River Pueblos, perhaps Taos to the north in New Mexico has become the best known, with its adobe buildings dominated by *Klauuma*, a five-storey block at the north of the Pueblo and virtually unchanged for centuries. Other villages, the names used to identify an individual's affiliation, are those such as Santa Clara, San Ildefonso and, just south of present-day Albuquerque, the largest of them all, Isleta.

To the west are the Pueblos of Laguna, Acoma, Zuni and Hopi. Classified as Desert Pueblos, the inhabitants were least influenced by Whites until recent years and in the case of the Zuni and Hopi, many of the old customs and ceremonials were still performed. Today, virtually all the Pueblos – be they River or Desert – are of great interest to visitors, especially for the many festivals such as that of San Geronimo in Taos and the Snake Dance of the Hopi, which are still performed annually to ensure fertility, rain and bountiful crops.

◀ The Pueblo of Taos in New Mexico showing the dominant five-storey block of *Klauuma*. Built entirely of adobe, the Pueblo has remained virtually unchanged for many centuries.

Navajo and Zuni silverwork

▲ The necklace, which is of Navajo design, is made of turquoise stones mounted in German silver and depicts a squash blossom motif. The small brooch (*contained within the necklace*) is of Zuni design.

The Southwestern tribes – Navajo, Zuni and Hopi – first learned the art of silverwork in the 1850s from Mexican smiths who came from the Rio Grande Valley.

The first pieces they made were crude and produced with homemade tools but with the passage of time, the work became more sophisticated and by the 1890s, most Pueblo people had their own silversmiths. Distinctive styles emerged from each of the tribes. Navajo silverwork is noted for its simplicity of design with large turquoise stones set within a silver mount. Zuni work is characterized by multi-layered inlays of shell and jet as well as turquoise, whilst the Hopi produce a style of engraved silverwork based on pottery designs and with only limited inlays. Shown here is a Navajo squash blossom necklace contrasted with a Zuni brooch on a silver chain.

Life in the Pueblos

Lifestyle in the Pueblos, outwardly at least, was similar. Monogamy was generally practised, the husband coming to live in his bride's home and descent was traced through the woman, the tribes being divided into mother-clans. Although government differed between the River and Desert Pueblos, both groups, to a greater or lesser extent, grew maize, beans, squash and sunflowers, domesticated the turkey and hunted both deer and antelope – sometimes buffalo. Clothing was mostly of cotton although in the north it was of buckskin. In historic times, the ancient yucca sandals were replaced by ankle-high, rawhide-soled moccasins and the robes of turkey feathers and rabbit fur, by woollen shawls and sashes. The usual Pueblo woman's dress at this time consisted of a rectangular *manta* or shawl generally of dark brown or black woollen cloth.

Pottery and basket work

The Pueblo tribes excelled in pottery, the style and designs embedded in the earlier traditions of their Hohokam, Mogollon and Anasazi ancestors, but progressively developed so that techniques of manufacture changed from mass moulding and sun dried to coiled, fired and polished. Each Pueblo generally produced distinctive styles, those from the Pueblos of Santa Clara and San Ildefonso being

particularly fine and still much sought after to this day by collectors.

Basketry too, legacy of an ageless art, was highly developed, techniques being of both coil and wicker types. Bear and other grasses, yucca, willow and devil's claw (*Martynia proboscidea parviflora*), both in natural and dyed shades, were used to produce trays, baskets, food vessels and even cradles for both practical and ceremonial uses.

◀ A pottery bowl from Isleta Pueblo in New Mexico. The black and red designs are typical of the region and are made of mineral or vegetable pigments. The pottery was constructed by the coil technique, building the vessel by coiling long rolls of clay into the desired shape.

▲ The Pueblo tribes excelled in basketry, both wicker and coil types being made. This sifter basket from the Hopi is made of split yucca leaves. It is of a style which was used in the region for hundreds of years.

Navajo weaving

By the mid-nineteenth century, the Navajo had become well known for the high quality of their weaving, producing distinctive blanket styles which differed from and were superior to those of their teachers, the Pueblo tribes, the ancient inhabitants of the Southwest. The craft was greatly encouraged by white traders in Navajo country who saw a ready market for the heavier woven blankets for use as rugs and floor coverings by non-Indians.

In the 1890s, so-called Germantown yarn was brought into the area which upgraded the quality of the wool employed in Navajo weaving. Vibrant red backgrounds were particularly popular with diamond and zigzag patterns in green, blue, yellow, pink, black and white. Styles varied throughout Navajo country, the so-called Yei rugs made in the Shiprock area display semi-realistic elongated figures (see page 46), which traditionally appear in Navajo religious sandpaintings, while those from the region of Ganado often have a cross design element, as shown on this piece (below) dating from the late nineteenth century.

▲ A Pueblo woman producing a tightly woven coiled basket of willow, wrapped with coloured grasses. For this art, which extends back thousands of years, a basketmaker must know the seasons for gathering the materials, how to harvest, dry preserve and prepare them for use, as well as knowing the various intricate techniques of construction.

◄ A Navajo design from the Ganado region dating from the late nineteenth century showing the traditional repeating cross and diamond pattern.

Kivas and Kachinas

Semi-subterranean ceremonial rooms, referred to as *kivas*, were a feature of most Pueblos. The traditional entrance was through the roof using a ladder. Here Society members and appointed priests set out sacred objects in preparation for days-long public ceremonials, the most complex of which centred around the *Kachina* cult. Here, masked and plumed members danced through the Pueblo to bring happiness to the inhabitants and reaffirm the promise of ample, life-giving rain.

▶ A Hopi priest costumed for the *Kachina* Dance in honour of departed relatives. The mask with its towering crest is a feature of the dance; the kilt – always woven by the men – is a traditional garment. The priest holds a gourd rattle in his right hand.

The Snake Dance

This ceremonial to bring rain, was held every two years by the Hopi Indians of Arizona, particularly in the Pueblos of Walpi, Mishongnovi, Shipaulovi, Shumopovi and Oraibi. Organized by the Snake and Antelope fraternities, the striking features of a complicated and largely secret rite were the gathering of snakes from the world quarters, the making of a sand altar and a ritual of washing the snakes. In public, the dancers form a line as shown here, holding snake whips of eagle feathers as well as prayer sticks. They wear deer hoof or tortoise rattles tied on the knee which are sounded, imitating the snake. A low chant begins which gradually intensifies in volume and at the same time, the lines sway in undulating curves. The dancers move towards the *kisi*, a small shelter which houses the snakes; here, they are given a rattlesnake which is grasped at its middle and held in the dancer's mouth. The dancer then moves four times around the plaza with the snake which is then returned to the *kisi*. The dancing concludes when all the snakes have been exhibited. In Hopi mythology, snakes were regarded as elder brothers and were thought to be powerful in compelling the nature gods to bring rain.

◀ An unmarried Hopi woman photographed about 1890. On reaching puberty, the girls dress their hair in whorls at the sides of the head, in imitation of the squash blossom, the symbol of fertility. Married women wore their hair in braids which was said to be the emblem of the ripened ear of corn.

▲ A Hopi *Kachina*. Such dolls were traditionally carved from the root of the cottonwood tree and represented the supernatural beings of the Hopi Indians, being used in the religious training of their children. The colourful sash illustrates that worn by the priest (*see far left, opposite*).

◄ A Hopi bullroarer. This was regarded as a prayer-stick of the thunder, the whizzing noise it produced as it was whirled around representing the wind that accompanies thunderstorms. It was traditionally made from a piece of wood riven by lightning. The tadpole motifs make reference to underwater spirits.

▲ Navajo silversmiths outside a *hogan*, traditional dwelling of the Navajo. *Pesh-lqakai-ilhini* (*left*) is hammering silver on a steel anvil.

This traditional *hogan* has a forked pole framework, covered with earth, reminiscent of Athapascan dwellings – original homeland of the Navajo.

The Navajo

Latecomers to the Southwest were Athapaskan-speaking tribes whose ancient homeland was far into the Subarctic north. Bands of these hardy, restless hunters and nomads, left the icy wastes of the north around AD1000 progressively drifting south. By about AD1600 one large group had settled adjacent to the Pueblo people, living in dwellings made of a wooden frame of three to five piñon logs, covered with earth and having a small extension at the entrance. A smoke hole was left at the centre of the *hogan* and the entrance always faced east, towards the rising sun. They referred to themselves as *Na-de'ne'*, 'The People', but the Pueblo tribes observing their lack of interest in agriculture, called them *apaches de nabahu*, 'enemies of the cultivated fields'! Today, known as Navajos, they are one of the largest and best-known tribes in North America, who rapidly adapted to their new surroundings, learning much – weaving, ceremony and religion, costume, social organization – from the indigenous Pueblo people, several groups of whom joined them after the great revolt against the Spaniards in August 1680.

Several aspects of Navajo mythology, religious beliefs and tribal thought were symbolized in their dry-paintings, produced using various coloured sands, pollens, dried and crushed flowers, charcoal and sandstone. Dry-painting altars figured prominently in healing ceremonials, their world view being that illness was due to the disharmony of an individual and his or her environment. The associated 'chant' or 'way', evoking the powers of the Navajo cosmos, was designed to effect a cure.

By the 1860s, the Navajo were pasturing large flocks of sheep and were growing corn, squash and melon. The *hogan* was still the main abode with adjacent corrals in which the sheep were kept every night. Horses were used for transportation and children were carried in cradles which were strapped to a wooden board.

Navajo weaving

Whilst blanket styles initially paralleled those of their Pueblo teachers, by the early 1800s the Navajo became increasingly known for their high-quality, finely woven and highly colourful blankets. At first, the process was entirely by hand – shearing, carding, washing and dyeing the wool, which was then spun using a wooden spindle. Early Navajo blankets were characterized by limited colours and simple striped patterns, often referred to as 'Chief's blankets'. Later, with the introduction of brightly dyed commercial yarn, patterns became more complex with large geometric designs. Navajo weaving began to decline in the late 1800s as commercial clothing became available from the traders but rather than allowing the craft to die out completely, the more reputable traders, such as Hubbell at Ganado, urged the Navajo women to make heavier blankets that would be suitable as

rugs for floor coverings. After much experimentation, rugs of high quality were being produced which had – indeed still have – wide appeal to a new, non-Indian market. Whilst almost all the designs were without significance, some traders did persuade the weavers to produce figures of the so-called *Yeibechai* spirits which were an ancient feature of a number of Navajo sandpaintings – although of no religious significance in the rugs.

Whilst Navajo weaving is still being carried out, the craft is really now more of an avocation rather than an occupation since a 5 x 3 feet (1.7m x 1m) rug, can take up to three hundred and fifty hours or more to produce. Sadly, since no weaver can obviously earn a living at the craft, with each passing year the quantity declines, although, reflecting pride in an ancient heritage, the quality remains exceptionally high. The tall Yei figures (*right*) were considered to be deities or invisible Earth Spirits and for many years it was taboo to weave them. With the apparent lack of retribution the patterns became popular!

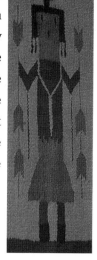

◀ A Navajo woman weaving on a blanket loom in front of a *hogan*, the typical habitation of the tribe.

The Apache

Until the close of the American Civil War, the intrusive Athapascans did more or less as they wished. They raided both Spanish and Pueblo settlements with impunity, capturing slaves as well as sheep, and then vanished into the numerous deep canyons where they were virtually impossible to find. At the same time they expanded their domain, which not only extended down into Mexico, but also completely surrounded the relatively peaceful Zuni and Hopi. The escapades of these swift and daring nomads could not be tolerated indefinitely and with the Civil War over, several New Mexico regiments, under the leadership of the famed Kit Carson, were put into the field against the Navajo and Mescalero Apache. Adopting a ruthless scorched earth policy – the sheep were killed, the peach trees cut down and the corn burnt – the tribes, first the Mescalero and then the Navajo, were forced into submission. By 1868, the Navajo signed a treaty acknowledging the authority of the United States; they agreed to settle, to take up agriculture and never to fight again. The 'long walk' of the *apaches de nabahu* was over.

Not so with such tribes as the Jicarilla, Lipan and Chiricahua Apache farther east. Practising little agriculture and herding no sheep, these people had been nomads for centuries, whose one source of livelihood and pleasure was raiding for livestock, guns, tools and cloth. Retreating to the craggy mountainous regions of southeastern Arizona, southwestern New Mexico and into Sonora, the Chiricahua had little use of horses. They lived in dwellings of brush which could be erected by the women within an hour. These *wickiups* were well adapted to the arid environment and nomadic existence and closely resembled those used by the tribes who lived in the Great Basin.

The Apache have gone down in history as amongst the bravest and cleverest of all Indian fighters, their chiefs such as Cochise and Geronimo

◀ A Jicarilla Apache. Like the Navajo, the Apache were relative newcomers to the Southwest. This particular Apache tribe spent much of its time on the Plains hunting with the Ute and Comanche. The eagle feather headdress seen here shows strong Plains influence, although the beaded brow band is obviously of Jicarilla origin.

The Apache girl's puberty ceremony

The puberty ceremony, which was referred to by the Apache as *na-ih-es*, was the celebration of the 'coming of age' of an adolescent girl after which she was considered an adult.

The ceremonial was performed to promote longevity, good physical and mental strength and prosperity for the girl. At the same time it reaffirmed kinship ties within the community, participants engaging in social dancing and singing. In the four days following the ceremony the girl was considered to be imbued with supernatural power and to have the ability to cure sickness and bring rain to the benefit of the community at large. For the ceremonial, the pubescent girl was provided with various items such as a crooked staff decorated with eagle and owl feathers, a drinking tube, scratching stick and a special woven basket which was used to dispense sacred pollen, symbolic of fertility. The most conspicuous regalia, however, was a beautifully embellished and fringed poncho and skirt as shown here in this early photograph; such items became coveted family heirlooms.

opposing submission for decades. Even as late as 1900, some bands still roamed free in the Chihuahua mountains of southeastern Arizona.

Geronimo was a Chiricahua Apache who, after years of fighting, finally surrendered in July 1886, so ending the Apache wars and effectively any further resistance in the west. A brave fighter and daring leader, he appealed to the more independent Apache people, encouraging them to continue their old, free way of life. They retreated to the Sierra Madre in Mexico where they carried on their raiding and hunting. The final penalty, however, was exile in Florida. Later they were moved to Alabama and finally to Fort Sill, Indian Territory, where descendants still live today. Geronimo survived until 1909, independent to the end and really rather enjoying life. He rode in the procession in honour of the inauguration of President Theodore Roosevelt and made some pocket money by selling photographs of himself and, on occasion, when demands were particularly pressing, brass buttons from his jacket.

PLATEAU AND BASIN: LAND OF HORSES AND FORAGERS

The in between land

Wedged between two rich cultural areas, the Great Plains to the east and the Northwest Coast to the west, the Plateau and Basin extends from the middle of British Columbia south to northern Arizona and New Mexico. Parts extend east into Montana and Wyoming, straddling the Continental Divide, whilst to the west are the Cascade and Sierra Nevada mountain ranges. It is a land of considerable contrast. In the north, particularly in Idaho and Washington, it is traversed by great riverways, such as the Clearwater, Salmon, Snake and Cascade – names hinting at either their character or products.

To the south, in the present states of Nevada and Utah, is an area of at least half a million square miles (1.3m sq km) which has limited precipitation, where no rivers drain to the sea and where most of the vegetation is sagebrush and saltbush clinging to a land largely composed of alkali plains, although in the north and east, in regions drained by the Snake and Green Rivers, there are impressive and beautiful grasslands with scattered forests of conifers on the higher ground.

Well into the nineteenth century, the human inhabitants of this region – described as the Great

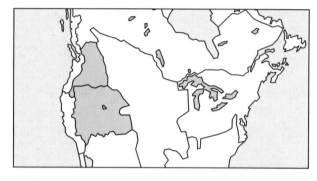

The Plateau and Great Basin cultural areas stretch from central British Columbia southwards to include the whole of Utah and Nevada.

Basin – carried on a lifestyle now known as Desert Archaic. This culture was developed more than ten thousand years ago and, although appearing simple, endured because of efficient and ingenious use of the region's natural resources, their bush shelters exactly matching – ventilation, protection from dust and sun – the desert environment. At first referred to dismissively by the Euro-Americans, their resourcefulness was later greatly admired.

◄ The valley of the Clearwater River, Nez Perce Reservation, Idaho. For centuries, the proud Nez Perce people lived in the well-water valleys of north-central Idaho, western Oregon and southeastern Washington. In the late nineteenth century, conflict arose as white settlers moved in to this beautiful land. Today, however, their descendants and the Nez Perce live side-by-side, both mindful of their heritage.

▶ A Flathead girl, daughter of Joseph LaMoose, an Indian scout. This fine-looking girl, photographed in 1913, the grand-daughter of a chief, is wearing a buckskin dress made by herself and her mother. It is of a typical Plateau style having a heavy beaded cape and fringed skirt. Note the tipi entrance in the background. Tipis were used on occasions by the Plateau tribes.

Bow-case and quiver

This is of a style popular amongst both the Plateau and western Plains tribes. Generally made of otterskin with the long quiver flap decorated with quillwork, later beadwork, the style was widely distributed and almost certainly originated amongst the Crow Indians with whom the Plateau tribes traded on the Yellowstone River. The bows, as shown here, were generally no more than 3 feet (1m) in length, arrows being up to 21 inches (53cm). Although the common form of Plateau bow was made of wood,

the finest were of mountain sheep or elk horn, generally two pieces being shaved down, spliced at the grip and given a heavy backing of sinew. The sinew imparted great elastic properties to the weapon, few having a weight (force required to pull the full length of the arrow) of less than 50 lbs (about 23kg) – powerful enough to drive an arrow completely through a buffalo! The horn bow was an important trade item. These bows were sometimes entirely covered with a snakeskin sheath, which not only decorated the bow but protected it from

damp. Other forms of decoration were with coloured cloth and braided porcupine quillwork, as shown (above) in the painting by the artist Karl Bodmer.

The people

Four major linguistic groups were represented in the Plateau/Basin cultural area. To the north were the Salishan-speaking Thompson, Okanagan, Shuswap and Lillooet; farther south in present-day Idaho and Washington were other Salishan speakers, such as the Coeur d'Alène, Colville, Kalispel and Flathead, whilst along the Columbia river ranged such tribes as the Yakima, Umatilla, Walla Walla, Nez Perce and Cayuse who were of the Sahaptin linguistic stock. Additionally, there were smaller groups such as the Kutenai in the

northeast, who spoke a language which has been identified as related to Algonquian. On the Lower Columbia there were Chinookan speakers where Chinookan was the basis of the so-called 'Chinook Jargon', a language which was widely used in trade and extended along the Pacific coast from California to Alaska.

The Basin area was dominated in the north of the region by Shoshonean-speaking tribes such as the Bannock and Shoshone. Further south the Paviotso, Paiute and Ute spoke a language which was related to Uto-Aztecan.

Population of most of these tribes seldom exceeded more than a few thousand, that of the Basin Ute, one of the largest tribes, for example, was estimated at four thousand in 1870, whilst the Plateau Nez Perce, probably one of the best-known tribes in this region, numbered in 1885, about fifteen hundred. War and disease obviously had a marked impact on these tribes since in 1805 Lewis and Clark estimated the Nez Perce population at about six thousand, whilst that of the Ute was, at the height of their power in the early nineteenth century, estimated at up to ten thousand.

Lifestyles
The Plateau region

Although gathering and hunting were important to all the tribes of this cultural area, one of the principal forms of subsistence of the Plateau people was salmon. The two great rivers, the Columbia and its tributary, the Snake, which run approximately north-south through the central Plateau region, abounded with this large and nutritious fish. Most villages, even small bands, had fishing rights along the streams and rivers where they used nets, weirs, spears or hook and line to catch vast quantities of the fish. The catch, which was often traded with interior tribes, was dried, then smoked on wooden racks to preserve it.

Some stretches of the rivers were particularly favoured as locations for catching salmon, thus the Kettle Falls on the Columbia, the highest falls on that river, were much used by the Colville, Walla Walla and Spokane, who built platforms which projected out over willow and stone weirs. Here, the salmon – impeded by the weirs – were speared using a specially constructed three-pronged wooden gig attached by a fibre cord to a long, 8 foot (2.5m) shaft. Sadly, this famous location no longer exists; this and other bountiful regions of the Plateau people now lie under the backwaters of the Grand Coulee Dam, which was constructed in the 1970s to produce electricity!

The Great Basin

Whilst the natural resources enjoyed by the Plateau people gave an abundant and relatively predictable lifestyle, that of the Basin tribes to the south was far less so. Here, a foraging economy based mainly on seeds and roots was the mainstay, being

▼ In contrast to the Plateau region, the country of the Great Basin tribes was, as shown here in Zion Canyon, southern Utah, mainly arid desert with scattered sagebrush and saltbush on the flats and piñon on the hills.

supplemented, for example, by the jack rabbit which was generally hunted in seasonal community drives. The pronghorn antelope was also found in limited numbers and, in the eastern part of the basin, tribes such as the Bannock and Shoshone had access to the Plains buffalo herds; indeed, until *circa* 1840, buffalo were to be found in their territory, west of the Continental Divide. The Basin tribes were, above all else, a remarkably practical and adaptable people and, even in such arid regions as central Utah and Nevada, they maximized the resources of the area. Great emphasis was placed on collecting root crops, such as bitteroot, camas, onion and potato, and for this reason the Great Basin people were referred to by the whites in the nineteenth century as 'Digger Indians', a derogatory description referring to their extensive use of digging sticks for prizing the roots and vegetables from the ground. In addition, they collected a wide variety of salad plants, such as wild lettuce, sweet cicely, violets and various brackens, supplementing their diet with fruits, such as chokecherries, wild grapes and elderberries. Pine nuts were one of their most important food crops. Locally referred to as piñon, these nuts were collected in the late summer and early autumn using long poles to dislodge the green cones. Transported in baskets to pits where they were roasted, the cones were then beaten to release the

▲ The temporary summer brush lodges of the Paiute (*above*) have been considered one of the most primitive habitations known to the North American Indian. They did, however, sustain the Great Basin tribes for thousands of years. More carefully constructed were their conically-shaped, rush-covered dwellings which were for winter use.

◄ *Ouray*, a chief of the Uncompahgre Ute, born in Colorado about 1820. He was noted for his unwavering friendship to the whites. This early photograph was taken by the pioneer photographer William H. Jackson about 1872. *Ouray* wears a heavily beaded jacket and leggings – typical Ute costume of this period.

seeds, these in turn being parched and finally the shells were separated from the seed by an elaborate and lengthy process of pounding and winnowing. The seeds could then be eaten in stews or soups but more frequently they were ground into a meal, moulded into cakes and dried in the sun. This method of preparation gave the tribes a product which, in the dry environment of the Great Basin, lasted indefinitely and could be used in times of want – a necessity in the unpredictable, often hostile, desert environment.

The piñon season was – indeed it still is – accompanied by much ceremonial; prayers were offered as thanksgiving for the first seeds and special dances performed. Whilst the piñon subsistence complex was one of the most significant features of the Great Basin cultural area, another was the communal grasshopper drives. Here, the ground was beaten with long branches, several areas being covered. The grasshoppers were progressively driven towards, and then into, a deep hole up to 12 feet (3.6m) in diameter. Thousands were caught this way, being a nutritious source of food: the largest were roasted, others made into a soup or, for future use, the bodies were crushed into a paste which was then dried. Perhaps more than anything, the grasshopper complex underlined the basic Great Basin philosophy, 'If it moves, it can probably be eaten'!

Mythology and religion

Considering the extensive amount of time spent in the quest for food, there is little wonder that in both their mythology and their religion, the Plateau and Basin peoples put great emphasis on the sacredness of life and had great reverence for the earth. There were extensive myths and legends which explained the origins of their staple foods – salmon in the north, piñon in the south, and coyote both as creator and trickster, dominated in tales relating to the origin of the earth, fire, the scattering of the tribes, even escapades with women! The most powerful spirits were – as with many North American tribes – the awesome forces of nature, dominated almost universally by a recognition of a supreme deity variously described as Our Father, Great Chief or Great Spirit. The Nez Perce world view emphasized the Sun as 'Father' and the Earth as 'Mother'. As the missionary, Kate McBeth, observed, 'All the products of the earth are children of the Sun, born of the Earth'. Throughout both the Plateau and Great Basin, there was great stress on the acquisition of spirit power through a vision or dream, the latter being more typical of the Basin tribes. In the Plateau region both boys and girls were encouraged to retreat to a remote spot to seek a vision; sometimes it took years for the desired spirit to be revealed and, even then, the results of the vigil were seldom disclosed until adulthood.

▲ The year 1838 saw the founding of a mission at Lapwai in the heart of Nez Perce country, built by the Rev. Henry H. Spalding in response to a Nez Perce delegation which travelled to St. Louis in 1831.
  Shown above is the tree into which is embedded an iron ring to which, it is said, uncooperative Indians were tied and whipped. The Park Ranger is David Rogers, a Nez Perce and a direct descendant of Chief Twisted Hair who met with Lewis and Clark in 1805.

Some individuals who had vivid or unusual visions became shamans, using their powers to help the tribe – by controlling the weather or predicting the location of game, for example. Unusually, in the Great Basin there were equal numbers of men and women shamans, although the women tended to use their powers only on other women.

Intrigued by new religions as early as the 1830s, Nez Perce delegations travelled as far east as St. Louis to encourage missionaries to bring Christianity to the Plateau people. Initially, conversions were successful – although not without some coercion – but the friendly contacts led to an influx of Whites and ultimately, in the last quarter of the nineteenth century, a clash of cultures which fractionalized the tribe. However it gave, historical immortality to two individuals – *Hinmaton-yalatkit*, 'Thunder-coming-up-from-the-water-over-the-land', better known as Joseph, a chief of the Nez Perce, and the prophet *Wovoka*, a Paiute from Pyramid Lake, Nevada (*see Powerful voices, page 56*).

The rendezvous

Trading was an important part of the economy of the Plateau tribes. One of a number of favourite gathering places was the so-called Dalles rendezvous on the Columbia River, which was held every summer reaching its peak in the autumn. Here, goods from far-flung tribes, not only from the Plateau and Basin but also from the Pacific Coast and Great Plains, were exchanged, each tribe specializing in materials which they knew would trade well with others. The Klamath specialized in the sweet and nutritious camas bulb; the Nez Perce in pipes, headdresses, horn bows, quilled or beaded clothing and buffalo robes (some of which they had obtained on trade excursions to the Plains tribes). The Nez Perce as well as the Palus also brought distinctively marked horses; the Wasco and Wishram, dentalium and other shells from the coast. Additionally, from these tribes and others came dried fish and meat, elk teeth, bear claws, fish oil, baskets, *parfleches* (*see page 54*), eagle and other feathers, cornhusk bags, and a variety of furs and animal hides – sea-otter and beaver being amongst the most prized. Various goods of white manufacture were also available, such as guns, brass and copper kettles, blankets and blue and scarlet cloth – which in early days were a luxury, but became essentials, making Indians increasingly dependent upon the products of the white man.

The appaloosa

The Nez Perce prized colourful mounts and their most valued horses were those which had great stamina and distinctive marking. Those that were white with black spots, probably raised from a few imported originals and then selectively bred, were considered the most valuable. During the nineteenth century, the Nez Perce horses were famous throughout the western country and east to the Dakotas. Many individuals were recognized as very effective stockmen, and herds of one hundred to five hundred horses were common.

The spotted horse, now referred to as an appaloosa, was valued at two or three times the worth of other horses and these were traded to the Plains tribes for buffalo products.

This picture, taken in 1952 by K. Engman, shows the Nez Perce girl, Amy Tilden, the granddaughter of Sam Tilden, a nephew of Chief Joseph, astride a superb appaloosa mount. Note the horse collar, beaded and embellished with red and blue cloth, and the bag across the front of the saddle with heavy buckskin fringes so favoured by the Nez Perce and other Plateau tribes.

Amy Tilden's buckskin dress has a solidly beaded cape with stars; motifs of this type were relatively common on Nez Perce costume, possibly influenced by the American flag.

▲ Amy Tilden, granddaughter of Sam Tilden who was a nephew of Chief Joseph of the Nez Perce, astride a superb and valuable appaloosa mount.

◄ Beaded forehead ornament for a horse. Such ornaments were widely dispersed in the Plateau and Basin region, many probably being obtained from the Crow as gifts or in exchange. This one is of rawhide embellished with beads and horsehair.

Arts and craft

The location of the Plateau and Basin cultural area, enabled them to draw artistic inspiration as well as materials from the coastal cultures to the west and the Plains cultures to the east. The result was a combination of the maritime and equestrian material cultures, but at the same time much emerged which was quite distinctive of the area.

It was the women who were the producers of all forms of clothing, did quill and beadwork, hide-tanning, made bags and decorated the *parfleches* with geometric designs. Men, on the other hand, fabricated objects of stone, bone, wood and horn, made the weapons and did realistic hide painting.

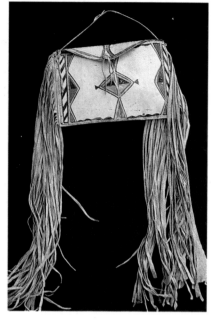

◄ A case made of rawhide and embellished with painted geometric designs on both flap and container. Often referred to as a *parfleche*, this style with the long heavy fringing was much favoured by the eastern Plateau and Basin tribes.

The cornhusk bag

A cornhusk bag, Nez Perce, *circa* 1890. The plateau tribes, Nez Perce in particular, were well known for the manufacture of flat bags which could be used for both storage and transportation. Such bags were made by twining without the use of a loom or frame. The warps and wefts were generally of hemp, although inner bark of the willow or elderberry was also used, the cord twisted by rubbing it across the thigh. Decoration was by means of a so-called 'false embroidery' where, as part of the weaving process, a strand of another coloured material – cornhusk was particularly popular in the nineteenth century – was wrapped around the weft each time it passed in front of the warp. Designs were always made up of geometric elements, repeated in rows and columns and were generally entirely different on each side of the bag. The decoration had no symbolic meaning, although some patterns were said to have been inspired by an American flag given to the Nez Perce in 1805, and they were quite different from those painted on *parfleches* (*far right*), generally exhibiting more complex design elements. It was customary at Nez Perce weddings for the bride's family to bring gifts of cornhusk bags filled with berries, camas bulbs or other edible roots, whilst the groom's family donated *parfleches* filled with shawls, calico, and blankets.

▲ A Nez Perce cornhusk bag dating from about 1890. This bag has a particularly tight weave resulting in sharp and well-defined designs, which are different on each side. The tight weave is a sign of a high-quality bag.

Traditional Plateau costume was made of soft-tanned deer or antelope skins, generally with the hair removed. The men wore soft-soled moccasins, breechcloth and leggings with perhaps a robe of elk or buffalo hide. On dress occasions, these were decorated with porcupine quillwork or beadwork, the appearance being similar to the costumes worn by such tribes as the Crow and Blackfeet, showing a definite Plains Indian influence. The women's costume consisted of moccasins, knee-length leggings and a long dress made of two large deerskins with open sleeves, the tail of the deer hanging at the throat. Additional decoration was in the form of beads, dentalium shells or elk teeth.

Influences from the Plains region progressively increased with the introduction of the horse in the early eighteenth century, and when trade expanded, many Plains tribes coveted Plateau products, such as cakes of berries and camas bulb, hemp twine, salmon oil, woven bags and horn spoons. In the same way, Plains products went to the Plateau, thus the traditional soft-soled moccasin was, towards the latter part of the

nineteenth century, replaced by the rawhide-soled type which was a style used on the Plains since the early 1800s. However, the soft uppers were generally embellished with a style of beadwork which tended to identify their Plateau origins, a general observation which can be extended to many other types of costume and accoutrements.

Distinctively Plateau, however, was the production of a variety of baskets and fibre bags and pouches. Best known of these was the so-called cornhusk bag, a flat container originally made from hemp cordage using a distinctive twining technique; the decoration was with various grasses, cornhusks and, later, coloured yarn. Generally used for storage and up to 3 feet (1m) in length, they were very popular trade items, being taken to the Plains country mainly by the Nez Perce who followed the famous Lolo Trail across the Rocky Mountains and who had strong links with the Crow Indians in the Yellowstone region.

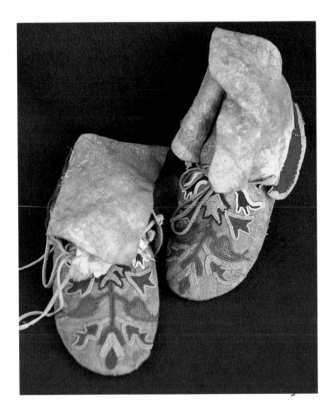

◀ A pair of woman's hard-soled moccasins decorated with floral beadwork of a style widely found on the Plateau particularly in the last quarter of the nineteenth century. Note the high ankle flaps embellished with red cloth which would go under the woman's knee-length leggings.

▶ Much of the Plateau Indian costume was greatly influenced by other cultures. Shown here is a military coat embellished with broad bands of pony beadwork in a style which suggests inspiration from the Blackfeet farther east. The coat was said to have formerly been the property of Chief Joseph.

Chief Joseph

In 1877, facing loss of land, loss of freedom, the very ethos of their lives threatened, nearly eight hundred Nez Perce – under such leaders as *Ollakot Too-hool-hool-zote*, 'Looking Glass' and *Hinmaton-yalatkit*, 'Joseph', – decided to leave their ancient homelands and seek sanctuary in the 'Grandmother's land' (Canada). Here, Sitting Bull had retreated after the Custer Battle a year previously and, it was said, enjoyed peace and fair treatment. So began one of the most epic retreats in North American history: a journey of nearly four months and some seventeen hundred miles, outmanoeuvring some of the best military strategists of the day.

But the Nez Perce never made it! Exhausted, and with over one hundred of their number dead, they finally capitulated in October 1877 at the Bear Paw Mountains, just forty miles from the Canadian border. Joseph – the only survivor of the able chiefs who had left Idaho four months previously – sent his surrender message to Generals Howard and Miles.

It was a message which for its dignity, eloquence and above all poignancy, has become for all time a tribute to the people he represented:

Hinmaton-yalatkit, Chief Joseph of the Nez Perce

'Tell General Howard I know his heart … I am tired of fighting. Our chiefs are killed … He who led the young men [Ollicut, Joseph's brother] is dead. It is cold, and we have no blankets. The little children are freezing to death … I want to have time to look for my children … maybe I shall find them among the dead. Hear me, my chiefs; my heart is sick and sad. From where the sun now stands, I will fight no more for-ever.'

Joseph never returned to his beloved Wallowa Valley and he died in 1904 – it is said, of a broken heart.

Powerful voices

By the mid-nineteenth century, the Plateau country was becoming increasingly subjected to white settlement as emigrants from the east sought new lands. The peaceful stance of the Plateau tribes towards the Whites had been exhibited some fifty years earlier when the explorers, Lewis and Clark, first visited the region in 1805 and then again, in 1831, when a delegation led by the young Rabbit-skin Leggings visited St. Louis seeking missionaries who would visit their country and tell them of a religion which they had been told was superior to theirs and that 'all would be lost if they did not embrace it'. Although all but Rabbit-skin Leggings died of diseases contracted in the white man's world, the endeavour was successful. By 1837, missions under the direction of Rev. Jason W. Lee, Dr. Marcus Whitman and the Rev. Henry H. Spalding had been established amongst the Bannock, Flathead, Cayuse and Nez Perce.

There was, however, dissent amongst the missionaries themselves, Protestant and Catholic missions competing amongst themeselves for Indian converts, which led to confusion and factions amongst the tribes. In 1847, the Cayuse, alarmed that they were being dispossessed, turned on the Whitman Mission, killing both Whitman and his wife together with ten other whites. The situation was later partially stabilized by the Isaac I. Stevens Treaty drawn up at the great Walla Walla

Council in 1855 which clearly defined tribal territory; it was to prove, however, an uneasy peace.

In 1877, conflict again erupted which resulted in the heroic retreat to Canada by many of the Non-Treaty Nez Perce (*see opposite*). The wars of 1877 all but silenced the Plateau people but not those in the Great Basin. Here, amongst such tribes as the Shoshone and Paiute, where strong religious impulses pivoted on death and regeneration, another form of protest arose.

This protest, which manifested itself in the form of a combination of native and Christian beliefs, led to the emergence of the so-called Ghost or Spirit Dance which was to sweep across the Plateau and Great Plains in the 1890s.

The Ghost Dance was initiated by the Paiute shaman and Holy Man, *Wovoka*, who lived near Pyramid Lake, Nevada. The dance was based on a vivid dream which he experienced on New Year's Day, 1889, in which God told him, he said, that if the Indians followed his instructions, a new world would be created. At first the theme was peaceful but progressively it became changed to satisfy the differing needs of the lawless tribes. In the case of the warlike and fiercely independent Sioux living in the Dakotas, which was more than a thousand miles away, it precipitated the death of Sitting Bull and the great tragedy of Wounded Knee, in December 1890 (*see Chapter 1*).

▲ The Paiute prophet, *Wovoka*, who on New Year's Day in 1889 had a vivid dream in which, he said, God told him that he must not lie or steal – must put away all practices which savoured of war and perform a particular dance – their reward would be a paradise on earth. The Ghost Dance swept the Plateau and Plains and led to the confrontation at Wounded Knee.

Tamason, Kalkalshuatash and Tuekakas

Tamason, was a member of a Nez Perce delegation to Washington, D.C. in 1868. In this early photograph by William H. Jackson he is wearing traditional Nez Perce ceremonial costume made of buckskin and mainly decorated with porcupine quillwork. He also carries a pipe typical of the Plateau tribe. *Tamason* was accompanied by *Kalkalshuatash* and other Nez Perce leaders to negotiate for reservation lands – the influx of white settlers leading to great tension between the two races. The Nez Perce had always been friendly to the Whites, including missionaries. *Tamason*, *Kalkalshuatash* and *Tuekakas* were three prominent leaders who were converted to Christianity, changing their names to Timothy, Jason and Joseph. *Tuekakas* became disillusioned by the influx of white settlers and left the mission to encourage Indians to adopt the philosophy of *Smohalla* and return to their old way of life, rejecting the teachings and things of the white man. Young Joseph (*see opposite*) was *Tuekakas's* son.

▲ *Tamason*, photographed by William H. Jackson in 1868 wearing ceremonial Nez Perce costume and carrying a pipe.

NORTHWEST COAST: LAND OF FORESTS AND WIDE WATERS

Of totem poles and potlatches

The Northwest Coast culture area extends from the Copper River delta on the Gulf of Alaska, south to the Winchuk River close to the Oregon-California border. Bounded on its west by the Pacific Ocean it extends inland following the crests of a series of mountains – the Chugach and Saint Elias range of southern Alaska and the Cascade range in Washington and Oregon. A long, narrow, crescent-shaped land over fifteen hundred miles (2,414km) in length, its widest point is about two hundred miles (322km), thinning to one hundred miles (169km) near the Winchuk River in the south.

Fronting a sea which is warmed by the Japanese Current and backed by high mountains which protect the region from the continental cold, the summers are cool and the winters wet and mild, a climate which has been likened to that of western Europe. Most of the coast is steep with little or no beach but with numerous rocky islands and inlets which penetrate deep into the mainland, giving an actual shoreline of almost ten thousand miles (16,100km). Very densely covered with forests of spruce and cedar, it was generally easier to travel by water than over land, the indigenous inhabitants being skilled boat-builders and bold seafarers.

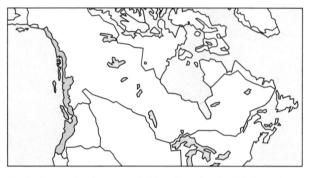

The Northwest cultural area extended from the panhandle of Alaska on the Pacific coast, south for some fifteen hundred miles to northern California.

The people

It is usual to divide North American culture areas into several regions; in the case of the Northwest Coast, the simplest subdivision is three – Northern, Central and Southern – differences such as art style, social and ceremonial traits, language and physical type, being apparent from one region to the next. Although not greatly different from other North American Indians biologically, there were an

◀ Northwest Coast terrain near the Fraser River in southern British Columbia. Two marine environments are found in this cultural area, an outer coast exposed to the ocean and, as shown here, an inner coast of numerous inlets of sheltered salt water heavily forested with spruce, fir and cedar.

◄ The Haida totems shown in this early photograph are in the village of Cumshewa. Positioned outside the houses of their owners, the smaller totems are mortuary or memorial poles marking the burial places of important members of the tribe. Totems were often carved from the trunks of red cedar trees.

unusually large number of languages, some forty in the historic period, belonging to at least a dozen language families. Further, whilst all other cultural areas in North America had a low population density, the Northwest Coast was, at the time of the arrival of Europeans in 1774, one of the most densely populated non-agricultural regions in the world, with some two hundred thousand indigenous inhabitants, although by the 1870s, because of little or no immunity to European diseases, the population had plummeted to less than forty thousand. In the Northern region there were such tribes as the Tahltan, Tlingit, Haida and Tsimshian; in the Central region, the Bella Bella, Bella Coola and

Kwakiutl, and in the Southern region, the Nootka, Cowichan, Chinook, Tillamook and Kusa.

Styles varied, but many of the tribes lived in enormous, gabled houses made of western red cedar planks, each holding eight or ten families. Several such houses, generally standing just above a river bank, constituted a village and outside some stood tall cedar poles, carved with figures, which made reference to the family or clan of the occupants. The front walls of the house might also be painted with bold, highly abstract figures, symbolic of animals – raven, whale, salmon, Thunderbird – which figured prominently in tribal mythology.

Tribal organization put great emphasis on status which was based on a combination of wealth and birth, the larger villages consisting of 'chiefs' or 'nobles' whose artificially deformed heads signalled their rank. Next came their followers (the 'commoners') and lowest of all, the slaves. Status was maintained by wealth, validated through formal gift giving during ceremonials and particularly at occasions referred to as *potlatches*.

As with other cultural areas in North America, there was also a widespread belief that human beings could acquire help from the non-human world, thus guardian spirits gave support to the healing shamans and harpooners; indeed, the acquisition of a guardian spirit was seen as the basis of success and skill in many endeavours.

◄ Many Northwest Coast tribes reshaped the heads of infants in their cradles. This woman, Ma-Ma Yockland, a Kwakiutl of the central coast of British Columbia, has a 'sugar-loaf' head, indicative of a high ranking individual.

► A Chinook youth. The Chinookan language furnished a major component of Chinook jargon, a trade language that was widely used throughout the Northwest. Trade with the Tlingit or other tribes farther north is evidenced by the wearing of the much coveted Chilkat blanket, a speciality of some of these northern tribes.

Arts and craft

The fullest expression of the Northwest Coast culture was to be found amongst those tribes such as the Tlingit, Tsimshian and Haida in the north. In particular, it was the Haida who were the major producers of the largest and greatest number of totem poles and who built the most imposing plank houses. The northern tribes also built the finest canoes and produced striking carvings on bowls, masks and chests. Whilst red and yellow cedar wood were the most widely used material, other media such as black argillite, copper and, later, silver were also employed. The metal was turned into various forms of jewellery which was often engraved with traditional totemic crest designs. Horn and bone were other important medias used in the production of ladles, spoons, clubs, toggles and the shaman's 'soul catcher', all of which were cut and shaped and then ingeniously carved, either in the round or as low-relief carvings.

Whilst pottery was absent, some of the finest baskets in America were made by the Coast tribes, three of the four major techniques – twining, plaiting and coiling – being employed, although the emphasis differed from one region to the next.

Woven blankets were also produced, the most valued – the Chilkat – being made by the Tlingit, Tsimshian and Haida, using an upright loom and combining spun cedar bark and mountain-goat wool in both weft and warp. Up to six feet (2m) in length and heavily fringed, they resembled the shape of an upside down house front, being two feet (0.6m) wide at the ends and three feet (lm) in the middle. They were worn only by high ranking individuals, the patterns represented the hereditary crests of their owners, a custom extended to body tattooing which, although widely practised on the West Coast, was most highly developed by the Haida.

▲ Some Northwest Coast shamans had, through the power of a supernatural helper, the ability to cure disease. An important part of the shaman's paraphernalia, was the 'soul catcher'. It was said that illness was caused by a soul leaving the body and this had to be enticed back to effect a cure. The 'soul catcher' shown here, which is possibly Tlingit, is a typical style being made of bone and elaborately carved.

◄ The ingenious technology in wood, so characteristic of the Northwest Coast tribes, is well illustrated by this painted plank house and totem poles, standing in the Tsimshian village of Kitwancool in northwestern British Columbia. The plank houses, which could be up to one hundred feet (33m) or more in length, were erected without the use of nails, the planks being tied together with cedar withes.

▲ Shaman's carved wood crane rattle, Tlingit/Tsimshian of the nineteenth century. The crane together with other birds was considered the shaman's spirit helper, as were the mountain goat and octopus, symbols of which are carved at the base of the human figure and around the sides of the bird.

▶ *Sitka Jake*, a Tlingit, wearing a Chilkat blanket. These magnificent five-sided blankets of cedar bark and mountain-goat's wool, were made by the women from tribes such as the Tsimshian, Tlingit and Haida on the northern coast. They were part of the sumptuous costume of high-ranking individuals in the *potlatch* and other ceremonials (*see also Chinook youth page 59*).

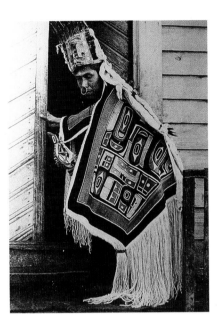

◀ In the early nineteenth century carvings using a slate-like soft stone as the medium and referred to as argillite, emerged as an important art form amongst the Haida of the Queen Charlotte Islands in British Columbia. Small examples of totem poles and house posts, as shown here, were carved and then the stone polished to give a high lustre. They became much sought after by Euro-American seamen as exotic souvenirs of foreign travel.

Tattooing

Many of the Northwest Coast tribes artistically embellished the human body. Commoners mainly used body and face paint while those of the higher classes, 'the nobles', practised tattooing, producing elaborate and more permanent forms of decoration. Tattoos were generally applied to the arms, legs, chest and back of men and the arms and legs of women but there were several notable exceptions to this rule. For example, powerful women shamans amongst the Tillamook of the Oregon coast, had an emblem of a mythical figure, Wild Woman, tattooed on their breasts, whilst high-ranking Haida women used emblems such as a stylized beaver or bear on the chest above the breasts, as shown opposite.

Tattooing was often done by a skilled specialist on the occasion of the *potlatch* (*see The potlatch, page 62*). Traditionally sharp thorns, spines of fish or small pieces of sharp bone were used, later needles obtained from white traders. Colours were invariably black, from finely powdered charcoal and red from Chinese vermilion. It was a lengthy process and sometimes designs were incomplete – if the work could not be finished during the *potlatch* or because of inflammation which the operation occasionally produced.

The Haida of the Queen Charlotte Islands of British Columbia were considered pre-eminent in tattooing, the marks being heraldic designs or the family totem of the wearers, similar to the carvings depicted on house and mortuary poles (*see The totem pole, page 65*). The complexity of the crests was impressive, requiring great skill and imagination, as shown in this Haida design (*above*) depicting a double raven and probably symbolic of membership of a Raven clan.

◀ Haida double Thunderbird design. Tattoo patterns are similar to those on house crests or totem poles.

▼ Tatooed Haida Indians. Such designs were heraldic or representations of the family totem or personal crests of the wearers.

The *potlatch*

'*Potlatch*' derives from the Chinook jargon word meaning 'give' and although the occasions for *potlatches* were numerous and varied greatly in importance, all were viewed as an activity which in different ways validated the social standing of a family or individual. The *potlatch* was performed by most of the Northwest Coast tribes from the Eyak on the Gulf of Alaska, south to the Chinook at the mouth of the Columbia River in what is now present-day Oregon.

Potlatchers gave, safe in the knowledge that the recipient would have to pay with interest: at some, valuable gifts were deliberately destroyed and those invited would, at some future date, be expected to reciprocate, if their social standing was to be maintained.

For this reason, *potlatching* has been described as a substitute for physical conflict; indeed, the Kwakiutl referred to the *potlatch* as 'fighting with property'. Both missionaries and white officials were often appalled at the quantities given away or destroyed, which sometimes left families destitute. For this reason the *potlatch* was, for a long time, officially forbidden by the Canadian government, the gatherings being banned in 1884 as part of the Federal Indian policy and remaining illegal until 1951. Needless to say, the law was frequently ignored and *potlatching* has continued up to the present day. Gifts changed with the times as European goods became increasingly available, thus a 1921 *potlatch* included engine-propelled boats, sewing machines, furniture, gramophones, even a pool table.

The Kwakiutl called their most important *potlatches*, *maxwa*, meaning 'doing a great thing'. Guests from other tribes were invited for the assuming of a chiefly name, a special feast, the buying and selling of the highly-valued engraved copper plates – referred to as 'coppers' – marriage or the ceremonial erection of a crest (totem).

Great ceremony and drama was associated with the display of the goods which were to be given away, the method of distribution being made according to the social rank of the recipients. It was a time for lengthy speech-making, special songs and dances together with dramatic theatrical performances, when the elaborate paraphernalia of Northwest Coast culture – masks, headdresses, special woven robes, ponchos, tunics and other regalia – was used to stunning effect.

The *potlatch* thus played an important role in passing on the tribe's cultural heritage from one generation to the next, for it was during the lengthy ceremonials that the children saw the dances and use of regalia and heard the traditional songs – all activities which referred to the legends as well as tribal and family history.

Shown here is a Kwakiutl group at Fort Rupert on the Queen Charlotte Strait, British Columbia, gathered around trade blankets which are to be distributed in a tribal *potlatch*.

Northwest Coast economy – the bountiful sea

The economy of the Northwest Coast was similar to that of adjacent parts of the Arctic, Subarctic, California and Western Plateau, depending heavily on fish, particularly salmon, halibut and sea mammals as a source of oil. The technology and pattern, however, differed somewhat throughout the area in the methods of hunting, fishing and gathering as well as the techniques of preserving the large quantities of food which became seasonally available.

A major source of food was the salmon and great salmon hunts were seasonally organized by most Northwest Coast tribes. So important was this fish to their livelihood, that in some Northwestern Indian languages, the word for 'fish' was simply the word for 'salmon', one scholar noting that this creature – which could be up to three feet (lm) in length – was as important to the Indian as bread to the white man. The enormous number of salmon caught in the seasonal hunts needed to be stored for future use and in a land where there was little sun and no ice, the only effective method of preservation was by smoking. The fish was cut open and spread apart with sticks; it was then placed on open topped racks with a small fire of alder wood underneath. It was careful work, the fish being left in the smoke for a week or so and to ensure that the inside of the flesh was also dried,

every day the split fish was softened by squeezing and rubbing. After the flesh had been thoroughly cured, it was folded up and stored away in baskets or bales for future use.

Another important fish, particularly to such tribes as the Makah, was halibut. These large fish were caught on lines set out on the banks some fifteen or more miles (24km) from shore. Special hooks were used which were attached to kelp (a long-stemmed seaweed) which was virtually unbreakable. The hooks, made of bent wood tipped with bone, were ingeniously designed and so beautifully shaped that they have been mistaken for ornaments.

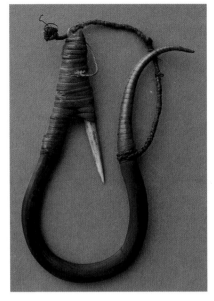

◄ A halibut hook, probably Makah. The hook is of a piece of bent hemlock with a sharp section of bone slanting from it which caught the jaw of the halibut when it attempted to take the bait. Because of the elegant shape, these hooks have sometimes been mistakenly identified as 'an ornament'.

▲ This basket was probably made by the Nootka tribe of Vancouver Island. It is constructed from split spruce root and uses a twining technique. The designs are worked in brown surf grass and show swooping birds and spectacular scenes, such as the hunting of whales in the open sea, for which the Nootka people were renowned.

The Nootka whale hunt – evoking the spirits

Whilst great skill, ingenuity and vigilance was required in capturing salmon and halibut, another important attribute – courage – was essential in the spectacular sea hunt for whales. Perfected by the Nootka of Vancouver Island – but also an activity of their neighbours, the Quileute, Quinault and Makah – the landing of a whale up to fifty feet (16m) in length, required more, the people said, than mere human strength. The hunt was turned into a highly ritualized, dramatic, event, summed up by the Makah whale harpooners' saying, 'If a man is to do something beyond human power, he must have more than human strength for the task'.

The harpooner, who was generally also the captain, was subjected to vigorous self-imposed training, much of which began at an early age. Paramount was the ability to dive and swim in deep, icy water, frequently imitating the actions of a whale – plunging, rolling and spouting. But the would-be whaler also required more than mere human ability and it was during a vigil, perhaps after a vigorous day's training, that the aspirant sought a supernatural helper which would give him unbeatable hunting power. A message from the stormy petrel, perhaps even the whale himself, was seen as signalling spiritual support and now the youth was convinced he could, with further effort, become a successful whaler.

▲ A Nootka whaler with harpoon. These were eighteen feet (6m) long and made of yew wood with a razor-sharp mussell shell point, barbed with elk horn. Attached to the shaft was an inflated sealskin designed to impede the wounded whale's progress and act as a buoy. The men were hereditary chiefs who occupied a position in the bow of the canoe during the hunt .

It was then that the young man began to acquire skills with the harpoon, learning from other more experienced men the quickness and alertness needed when facing a whale on the open sea. Whilst crew members, steersman and paddlers were obviously important to the success of the hunt, the skill of the harpooner was vital. The harpooner's carefully designed weapon was up to eighteen feet (6m) in length, its ingenious virtue being a detachable head of carved elk horn into which was set a razor-sharp point made of mussel shell. On striking the quarry, the head separated from the shaft whilst a lanyard of whale sinew (wound with nettlecord to keep it dry), connected to the head now deeply embedded in the lungs or heart of the whale, prevented its escape. As the whale resurfaced, other canoes approached and more harpoons were plunged into its massive body. The exhausted creature was finally despatched with a special chisel-head lance: it was a frightening, spectacular and bloody battle which required great courage and skill on the part of the whalers – little wonder that they also needed the support of their guardian spirits.

Amidst a great ceremonial welcome, the carcass was eventually beached and the exalted harpooner oversaw the distribution of the meat. Prized portions such as the blubber, a rich source of oil, were given to the crew, the remainder to the assembled crowd. Now a great feast was held, organized by the chief and his wife, and honouring the spirit of the whale.

These great whale hunts, man against nature and the evoking of spiritual powers, must stand as a tribute to the fearless seafaring people who occupied the Northwest Coast long before the arrival of Europeans.

The totem pole

Although commonly referred to as totem poles, the term 'crest pole' is probably the more accurate since the figures carved on them make reference to the owner's hereditary ancestors. The pole was, in reality, an heraldic device being a visual record of the social position and history of the family lineage. Totem poles were never part of religious ceremonials and they were not, as is sometimes mistakenly thought, worshipped. The early photograph shown at the top of page 59 is probably of the Haida village of Cumshewa and illustrates the positioning of the poles outside the houses of their owners. The smaller ones are mortuary or memorial poles adjacent to the burial of some prominent tribal member.

Totem or crest poles were carved from the trunks of the red cedar tree and reached their peak amongst the northern tribes such as the Haida, Tlingit and Tsimshian, in the period from 1850–1900, their development being stimulated by the availability of European tools.

Before undertaking the formidable task of carving the giant cedar into the complex figures found on the crest or totem poles, the carver made up a *maquette*, enabling correct placement and scale to be established and agreed upon. Such models were themselves works of art, that shown here on the far right, which is probably Kwakiutl, being a good example. Without a knowledge of the family, it is not possible to get a precise interpretation of the heraldry involved; however, the figures shown on this carving seem to depict a stylized raven, a bird recognized for its cleverness and cunning. In the middle is a salmon which figures in much tribal mythology and a bear revered because of its awesome powers. By the mid-nineteenth century Northwest Coast artists, responding to the obvious intererst of Euro-Americans, created a variety of objects for sale, the majority of which were imaginative extensions of native traditions, such as depictions of the mythical Thunderbird (*right*).

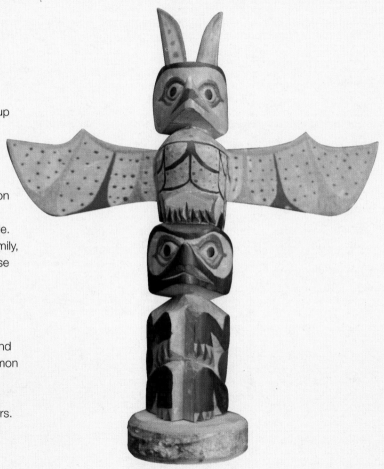

▲ Kwakiutl totem pole. The winged figure represents the Thunderbird, particularly important in Kwakiutl mythology. Poles of this style were erected over graves or in front of plank houses.

▶ Carved maquette, probably Kwakiutl, showing figures – birds, salmon, bear – which were prominent in tribal mythology and heraldry.

CALIFORNIA: A BOUNTIFUL LAND

A land of diversity and harmony

Bounded by the Sierra Nevada-Cascade range to the east and the Pacific Coast to the west, the Californian cultural area was peopled by a multitude of small 'tribes' all of whom occupied one of the most productive and bountiful areas of the world. The coastline stretched for nearly one thousand two hundred miles (1,931km) from the Arctic in the north to the Lower Sonoran Desert in the south. One notable climatic exception is the Mojave Desert, with an annual rainfall of less than seven inches (17.5cm).

The diversity of terrain modified lifestyle, so the California culture area is generally divided into three regions – southern, central and northwestern. Here the indigenous peoples lived in almost perfect conditions for primitive man, with lakes, rivers and marshlands teeming with fish and wildfowl, the land abounding with elk, deer, squirrels and rabbits, while along the western coast the Pacific ocean was rich in fish, abalones, clams, mussels and crayfish. Famine was unknown, horticulture unnecessary and with the vastness and rich resources of the region and its small population – perhaps 150,000 when the first white people arrived – there was little nomadism and limited inter-tribal warfare.

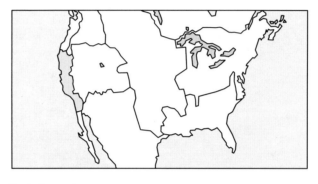

The California cultural area with a coastline of nearly one thousand two hundred miles from the Arctic in the north to the Lower Sonoran Desert in the south.

◄ The beauty of the Californian habitat, home to countless tribelets of the region, is illustrated by this scene near Sequoia.

The people

The original inhabitants of California lived in numerous, but often relatively isolated, village communities, which seldom exceeded more than 300 inhabitants. The political organization rarely extended beyond the village and such groups were generally referred to as 'tribelets', rather than tribes.

Dialects differed markedly from one village to the next, such that over one hundred different languages have been identified belonging to six distinctive linguistic stocks, a variation so great that the Californian cultural area ranks amongst the largest aboriginal linguistic diversity in the world. Dominant, however, were two linguistic stocks, Hokan and Penutian, but others, together with their numerous dialects, were scattered throughout the region and included, particularly, to the north, Algonquian, Siouan, Athapascan and Shoshonean. Little wonder that California has been described as a haven for the wanderers and a seducer of migrants! Such a pattern would be repeated by the white emigrants who, after about 1840, swarmed into the region and eventually became the dominant race.

House types varied considerably throughout the region. In the south, amongst such tribes as the Diegueño, Cupeño, Cahuilla and Luiseño, the usual habitation was a conical structure up to 16 feet (5.5m) in diameter and 9 feet (3m) high. This was made with six or more poles set into a circular formation, the sharpened ends being thrust into the ground; lighter saplings were set between these. The tops of the poles were then drawn together and secured with a cordage of wild hemp. Other poles running horizontally were tied to the uprights and

▲ The habitations of the Californian Indians varied considerably. This one is made of earth and was used by members of the Koso, a Western Shoshone band who lived in southeastern California.

Gatherers and foragers

The way of life of the Californian tribes was embedded in an ancient culture, heavily dependent for subsistence on seed gathering and foraging for tubers and roots. Young grasshoppers and caterpillars were also eaten and considered to be great delicacies. Deer and rabbits were hunted and the river and sea provided fish, mussels and clams – sometimes otters and seals – as the Californian Indian wandered over a wide circuit, gathering just about every edible thing which he could find.

The piñon nut was an important source of food and its harvesting was sometimes accompanied by great, cult-like ceremony. The Tipai of Baja California performed the Piñon Bird Dance, so named for the jays which noisily congregated in late autumn when the seeds ripened! The staple diet was the acorn which, after leaching out the bitter tannic acid, made a nutritious mush when mixed with water and eaten with caterpillars, which were parched in a basket. Here, Cecilia Joaquim, a Pomo woman, is collecting seeds in a close-twined burden basket.

then this frame was thatched with bunches of grass and reeds, which were tied to both cross poles and uprights. Sometimes the house was earthed part way up and there were generally two entrances about 2½ feet (0.75m) high at the south and north. Other semi-permanent dwellings were also used during the hot summer months or on hunting trips and these were made with tule (bulrush) mats over a framework of poles, generally without a roof. In central California, amongst such groups as the Yuki, Pomo and Yokuts, houses were also conical in shape but often covered with bark and, unlike those to the south, generally had a smoke hole at the top. Other habitations were semi-subterranean, covered with earth, or multi-family roundhouses, the frame thatched with grass or tule. Although the material scene remained similar – fish, venison and acorns were still the staple diet – houses in the north, such as those of the Hupa and Yurok, were now of large sheets of cedar planks with a pitched roof and sunken floors, a style much influenced by the Northwest Coast tribes.

The gathering complex

As in the Plateau and Basin region, all the Californian tribelets were gatherers as well as hunters and fishermen.

The gathering complex included a wide range of fruits, nuts, grass seeds, roots, tubers, bulbs, and various greenery. However, paramount throughout the region was the harvesting of acorns, which were collected in the autumn. The most prized were those from the tan oak, but other species were also collected. It was a joint task, the men and boys climbing the trees to shake down the acorns, and the women gathering them in large conically-shaped baskets. The acorns were then shelled, split, dried and stored to be used as needed. They were generally pounded into a meal before use, the bitter tannic acid was leached out by pouring warm water through the meal, which was placed in a porous basket or simply in a depression in the ground. The highly nutritious acorn meal was eaten as a type of porridge, made into a soup, or

◄ Acorns were an important part of the Californian Indians' diet. They were stored in special granaries made of wood and straw. Others, such as this Diegueño granary, were used to store mesquite beans.

into cakes, generally being combined with berries, meat and various other ingredients from nature's bountiful crop – nothing was cultivated except a little tobacco. Cooking was achieved by the use of hot stones dropped into a tight woven basket or into a hole lined with an untanned skin.

In this genial climate, clothing was quite simple. Men frequently dispensed entirely with clothing or wore a simple apron of deerskin. Women, however, were never seen without double aprons of fringed buckskin, fibre cordage or shredded bark. These were generally shorter at the front than the back. During cold weather, or on ceremonial occasions, robes of rabbit skin or – for the wealthy – otterskin,

were worn and although they often went barefoot, they sometimes wore sandals of yucca or twisted agave fibre, or a type of deerskin sock.

Transportation was mainly by dugout canoe or raft; however, the seagoing Chumash of the Santa Barbara coast, built the only New World's planked boats. Capable of carrying up to twenty people and sometimes more than 20 feet (6m) in length, they were made of planks split from driftwood which were lashed together with fibre cords and the seams caulked with asphalt; they were propelled by double-bladed paddles, sail power being unknown. Seafaring was important to the Chumash who depended on sea food as their main source of food.

▲ A Karok warrior of northern California. He is in war costume which consists of a tunic of rod armour and heavy deerskin apron. The bow could be a deadly weapon at close range – note the great length of the arrows in comparison to the bow.

Ishi: the last wild Indian in North America

Ishi was the survivor of the Yahi tribe of northern California. In 1908 the last village of the Yahi was discovered; treated virtually as vermin by many settlers, the Yahi fled in terror – only Ishi, the Yahi word for 'man', survived. Two and a half years later, Ishi exhausted and alone, stumbled into the white man's world – and was astounded that it did not lead to his immediate death! Ishi was taken in tow by two anthropologists at the University of California where he worked as a janitor in the Museum of Anthropology. Ishi was a master of the skills of his tribe and willingly demonstrated them as well as imparting his knowledge of the beliefs and language of the Yahi people. When he died of tuberculosis in 1916, he left an invaluable record relating to the tribes of California and had gained the affection and respect of all those associated with him. The skills Ishi demonstrated were essential for survival in his Stone Age culture: such skills as the Yahi techniques of fire-making, the production of arrows, harpoons and deer snares and the methods of adzing (carving) juniper wood for a bow. Also, the flaking of obsidian (dark, glassy volcanic rock) for arrow and spear points – even 'calling' rabbits.

Basket and featherwork

As basket-makers, the Californian Indians were without peer, with the women of the Pomo tribe standing supreme. A variety of coiling and twining techniques were used and in addition to the everyday utensils, special containers – generally elongated – were fabricated for rituals. These were embellished with elaborate, rhythmic, geometrical designs; others were studded with shells or brilliant feathers from the heads of woodpecker, hummingbird or quail.

▼ A hat woven of various roots and digger pine fibres was a feature of the Shasta tribes of northern California. Californian Indians were amongst the finest basket-makers in the world.

Featherwork was a particularly important part of ceremonial regalia; most elaborate were beautiful headbands of flicker (woodpecker) and other feathers, testimony to the owner's status and the abundance of bird life in the region. Condor feathers – the bird being particularly revered – were worn by such tribes as the Yurok and Hupa in the north. Often pieced together to produce a feather up to nearly 2 feet (0.6m) in length, they were worn in the White Deerskin, Jumping, Big Head and other dances which generally put emphasis on evoking the higher powers for world renewal, as well as on a display of wealth and status.

The Californian tribelets indeed lived well. Little wonder that, to the white man, the region was a paradise gained! Now, for those of the indigenous population who survive on the numerous tiny reservations scattered throughout the area, it is a paradise lost forever.

World renewal: the White Deerskin Dance

A major cult system which put emphasis on world renewal was an important facet in the lives of the tribes of north-western California, such as the Yurok, Hupa and Karok. Two distinctive ceremonials were associated with this cult, referred to as the Jumping Dance and White Deerskin Dance; their origins were explained in tribal mythology which was recited by a high-ranking person prior to the commencement of the ceremonials. The White Deerskin Dance involved the ceremonial use of an elaborately embellished tanned hide from the rare albino deer, which was symbolic of birth, the importance of the male and evoked the spirit of the deer for the benefit of the tribe.

As can be seen here, the participants wore headdresses decorated with woodpecker feathers attached to a band of tanned deerskin which had been removed from the animal's belly. In such dances they also carried tubular bone purses (below) and, as a sign of wealth, they displayed beautifully chipped blades of obsidian (a dark, glassy volcanic rock), enormous decorated pieced-together feathers from the mystic condor and a variety of bone and shell, particularly dentalium (below left).

◄ Strings of dentalium shells and beads. The shells were a rare, difficult type to find and were particularly coveted as a form of currency by the Californian tribes.

◄ An elkhorn purse closed with a strip of carved bone, held in place with a fibre thong. Such containers, as shown here, were generally elaborately etched. They were used to hold the coveted dentalium shell currency (see left).

SUBARCTIC: LAND OF THE SNOWSHOE AND CARIBOU

The great lone land

Spanning a vast area from Alaska in the west to the Labrador peninsula in the east – including the island of Newfoundland – the Subarctic culture area dips below the southern shores of Lake Winnipeg and the Hudson Bay; in total, it encompasses an area of some two million square miles (5m sq km). Sparsely populated with both Algonquian – and Athapaskan – speaking peoples, it is largely a land of numerous low-lying lakes, bogs and streams although to the west in the foothills of the Rocky Mountains in northern British Columbia, it becomes mountainous and rugged. To the south, the landscape is dominated by enormous forests of coniferous trees, such as pine, cedar, spruce and larch, whilst in the north it changes to more open woodland and then tundra where it borders on the Arctic. The tundra – often referred to as the Barren Grounds – was home to countless thousands of caribou which were vital to the lifestyle of the indigenous human inhabitants, particularly the Chipewyan.

The tribes who occupied this vast region were thinly scattered; indeed, it has been estimated that at the time of arrival of the first Europeans in the mid-eighteenth century, the population was no more than 60,000.

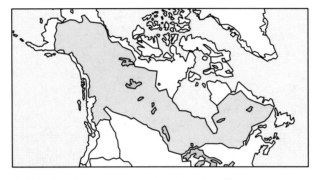

The Subarctic culture area spans a region of about two million square miles from Eyck near the Pacific shore to the Montagnais on the Gulf of St. Lawrence.

The tribes

Tribes of the Algonquian linguistic stock, with numerous dialects, were the Cree, Northern Ojibwa, Saulteaux, Naskapi and Montagnais, whilst more to the north and west, the Athapascans were represented by such tribes as the Tanaina, Kutchin, Ahtna, Yellowknife, Dogrib, Beaver and Chipewyan – to name a few. The tribes lived in small bands for much of the year, really no more than extended

◀ Caribou, essential to the sustaining of life amongst such tribes as the Chipewyan of the Subarctic tundra. The animal provided not only sustenance but skins for clothing and bone and antler for tools.

family groups and largely isolated from one another, the emphasis on lifestyle was one of great individuality and independence, tribal cohesion being minimal.

Lifestyle and mythology

Although the overall lifestyle throughout the region was similar, for example no agriculture was practised and all were hunters, fishermen (and later trappers), there were considerable differences in the style of dwelling used, method of transportation, warfare patterns and attitudes towards the care of the elderly. A marked feature of the Subarctic culture was the great emphasis placed on personal freedom but tempered with respect for others – an essential trait to ensure that harmony was maintained in the close-knit extended families which generally constituted the band. This gave rise to individuals who displayed a high degree of self-reliance and independence. Another Subarctic trait, obviously developed from an appreciation of the consequences of extreme isolation, was a mythology which referred to lone prowlers, such as cannibals with hearts of ice, lost souls who became rejected because they strayed too far from other humans. Subarctic mythology also reflected the precarious existence of humans in what was often a hostile and unpredictable environment, serving to establish a proper code of behaviour in social interaction, ritual, and the correct use of natural resources. One great priority in ritual, which evoked mythological beings, was to encourage an increase in game animals.

The snowshoe

The snowshoe was probably invented in the Old World and introduced to North America by white traders and trappers. Its subsequent use, particularly by the tribes of the Subarctic region, enabled the development of cultures which would otherwise have been impossible because of the way movement was restricted in the deep snow.

The main parts of a snowshoe are the wood rim, heel and toe cross piece, also generally made of wood, and a webbing of rawhide or twisted sinews referred to as *babiche* – a word derived from Micmac meaning 'cord' or 'thread'.

The 'snowshoe complex' gave rise to an increased exploitation of natural resources by the Subarctic tribes: the style of snowshoe, however, varied considerably depending upon the nature of the terrain and snow density. Amongst the Montagnais-Naskapi of the Labrador region, they were broad and oval, sometimes almost round, whilst in the west amongst such tribes as the Chipewyan and Swampy Cree, they were long and narrow. Types were often identified according to the familiar shapes which they resembled, such as Swallowtail, Beaver Tail or Bear Paw.

▼ The broad, oval-shaped snowshoes typical of the Montagnais-Naskapi of the Labrador region.

▶ Tribes in the west of the region, such as the Chipewyan and Swampy Cree wore long, narrow snowshoes.

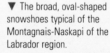

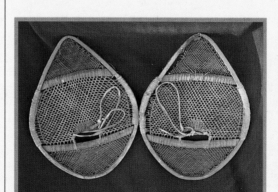

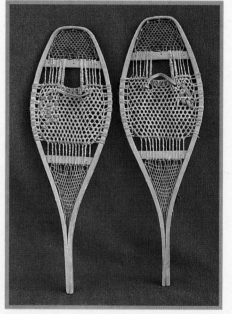

◄ Chief *Stickwan*, leader of an Athapaskan-speaking Lower Ahtna band who lived in the Copper River valley of southern Alaska. Note his fine shell and bead necklace, a very popular item of the Subarctic region.

caribou, moose or hare shoulder blade bones were held over a fire. As the bone cracked and blackened, it made complex patterns on the surface and these were then interpreted by the story-teller linking the patterns with myths, legends, or foretelling the future – the complexity of the tale being in direct proportion to the imagination of the practitioner!

Scapulimancy was an ancient custom and has been sustained throughout the years. It was first described by a Jesuit missionary in the early seventeenth century and was actually filmed in process by Hugh Brody in an Eastern Montagnais camp on Goose Bay, Newfoundland, in the autumn of 1989. Bones of animals were also carefully cleaned and often saved to be used as tallies or talismen and were also regarded as a way of honouring the spirit of a particular animal.

◄ A Sekani medicine man. His heavy blanket coat is wrapped at the waist with a colourful and widely used *ceinture fléchée* (sash), finger-woven from woollen yarn. The hair style is typical of many of the Subarctic tribes and is generally, as shown here, held in place with a headband. For special occasions these were often highly decorative (*see below*).

Scapulimancy

During the long winter months, particularly in January and February, outside activities were virtually impossible due to the extended hours of darkness and the intense cold.

It was during this period, within the warmth of the Subarctic dwelling, that the story-tellers recounted the myths, legends and history of the tribe. An important aid to the Montagnais-Naskapi shaman or medicine man of the region, was the employment of scapulimancy, a ritual where

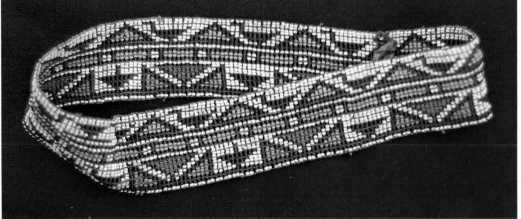

◄ A Montagnais-Naskapi woven beaded headband dating from about 1900. Such headbands were used on ceremonial occasions and generally displayed – as shown here – patterns of mountains, hills and birds mainly worked in red and blue beads on a white background.

The Cree

One tribe, the Cree, were dominant in the Subarctic, ranging from south of the Great Lakes, west to the Great Plains and east to the Labrador peninsula, the various bands being identified by their location, such as Western Woods Cree or Swampy Cree. The Woods Cree were masters in the use of light portable canoes and lived in conical dwellings, both being fabricated from birch bark. The abundance of fish, large game animals, such as moose and caribou, and wild berries permitted some population concentration in the spring and summer months which enabled socializing with other bands, the reinforcement of social ties and the forward planning during the winter dispersal; it was a pattern of lifestyle which was widely recognized throughout the Subarctic region.

The costume of Cree men consisted of leggings, breechclouts (a type of loincloth) and moccasins made of tanned hides of the elk, caribou or moose. The upper part of the body was covered with a shirt or coat which almost reached the knees. Additional clothing consisted of a cloak of beaver, caribou or otter skin with the hair left on. Women wore long dresses of moose or elk hide which were generally belted at the waist. Often they had detachable sleeves which were tied to the dress with thongs and could be removed during warm weather. The clothing of the children was similar to that of the parents although often, for additional protection especially in winter, they wore caps made from animal pelts (later cloth or wool) and mittens lined with fur. Such costume, especially for festive occasions, was embellished with painted designs, porcupine quillwork or, later, when white trade goods became available, beads and silk thread.

▶ A chief of the Woods Cree with the Hudson Bay Trader, Philip Godsell. The costume worn by this chief shows influence from the Plains tribes to the south – such as the eagle feather headdress and beaded shirt. The floral beadwork and moccasins, however, reflect much of Subarctic regalia.

▲ A Montagnais summer encampment photographed in Labrador about 1900. The Montagnais lived in a variety of dwellings, those for winter use might be earth-covered to insulate from the severe climate, but others, as shown here, were conically-shaped tipi structures covered with rolls of birch bark.

The Athapaskans: strangers in the north

Tribes belonging to this linguistic stock, such as the Tanaina, Kutchin, Tanana, Tahltan, Hare, Yellowknife, Beaver and Chipewyan, to name but a few, were members of one of the largest indigenous linguistic groups in North America. They inhabited a vast region of the Subarctic cultural area stretching from the western interior of Alaska to the western shores of Hudson Bay. Their neighbours to the north were the Eskimo, the Eastern Woodlands and Plains tribes to the east and south, and the Indians of the Plateau and Northwest Coast to the west and south. Other Athapaskans, such as the Navajo and Apache, are represented in the American Southwest, descendants of people who migrated there in the fourteenth century.

The term 'Athapaskan', with its variety of spellings, is an Algonquian word used by the Cree to refer to the 'strangers' who lived to their north – a land which had areas of great beauty but in other parts was bleak and inhospitable. Here, for thousands of years, these adaptable and resourceful Native Americans have made their homes, their annual cycle of activities regulated by the dictates of the season, but more than anything they were closely aligned with the migration patterns and abundance of game which was so vital to their subsistence.

Woven quillwork

In the historic period, some of the finest quillwork was produced by the Cree, Northern Athapascan tribes, the Iroquois and the Indians of the Great Lakes. The work was carried out on a single loom of the type shown here (*below right*). This form of decoration has the appearance of being made up of fine cylindrical beads but in reality it is composed of small, dyed and flattened porcupine quills which have been woven in between the warp threads, passing over and under the crossing elements. Owing to the limitations of the technique, all the designs are geometrical. However, very striking patterns are produced with tasteful combinations of colour. The work is still carried out by a few Indian women in the vicinity of Fort Providence on the Great Slave Lake in the Northwest Territories of Canada. Christine Minoza (*above right*) is shown working at a piece of weaving and using a loom virtually identical to that shown here (*right*). The finished bands are used to decorate jackets, gun cases, gauntlet gloves or mitts and belts.

◄ Christine Minoza, an Athapaskan woman of Fort Providence in the Northwest Territories, photographed about 1977 working on a quillwork band using a loom (*see below*). Only a few women now undertake this intricate type of quillwork which requires great patience and skill and is distinguished by its delicacy and beauty.

◄ A partially finished piece of loom beadwork collected at Fort Providence in 1978, which clearly shows the weft and warp threads, the latter spaced with stiff pieces of polythene. In early days this spacer would have been made of birch bark.

Floral beadwork

The beadwork of the Subarctic peoples from the early nineteenth century onwards, consisted predominately of beautiful floral designs. There is considerable evidence which suggests that such work was introduced to the Subarctic tribes via the European embroidery tradition by various non-Indian women, such as nuns, minister's wives and teachers, who sought to influence the native women in the 'ways of civilization'. Nevertheless, building on the more traditional foundations of designs and techniques in both porcupine quillwork and moosehair embroidery, a distinctive style of work emerged and examples from many of the Subarctic tribes – such as from the Slave, Dogrib, Chipewyan, Kutchin and Cree – are quite characteristic. Wall pockets, dog blankets, mittens, moccasins, gun cases, firebags, belts used for carrying babies and the like were embroidered with tasteful combinations of colour in both realistic and semi-realistic designs, generally on a trade cloth with background colours of red, black or blue. Shown here is a shelf valance which is similar in style to that used in earlier days for a drum cover. It was probably made by Cree Indians in the vicinity of Prince Albert, Saskatchewan, *circa* 1890.

Decorative Arts

Trade goods, such as beads, dyes, coloured wools and silks, made a great impact on the artwork of the Subarctic peoples. Prior to their introduction, in common with several other cultural areas, natural materials such as porcupine quills and shells were used. Most popular and widespread was the use of the dentalium or tusk shell, so called because it resembled in shape an elephant tusk. Some two inches (5cm) in length, it was a coveted trade item and used in the embellishment of clothing, generally in combination with blue or black beads. Dentalium shells were also very popular in the production of necklaces and carrying straps, often in combination with pieces of abalone or other iridescent seashells.

Whilst large areas of clothing could be covered comparatively quickly with dentalium shells, it was an exceedingly expensive form of embellishment; thus, one trader reporting from the Yukon in 1847, said that he could get one beaver or three marten hides for just six or eight shells and that a box of the shells would be worth 'over two thousand pounds'.

Far less expensive was the use of porcupine quills which were either sewn direct to the surface of buckskin or used on a loom, long bands being produced which could be used to embellish shirts, leggings and dresses. Some of the finest loom quillwork was, indeed still is, made by the Slave and

Dogrib people who live in the vicinity of the Great Slave Lake in the Northwest Territories. Time now, not cost, was the crucial factor in the manufacture of this exquisite work, it taking a whole day to produce about two and a half inches (6.25cm) of belt width. Little wonder that beads, as used by the Naskapi in the production of their headbands, became more popular later.

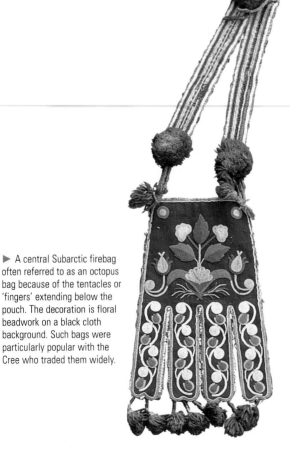

▶ A central Subarctic firebag often referred to as an octopus bag because of the tentacles or 'fingers' extending below the pouch. The decoration is floral beadwork on a black cloth background. Such bags were particularly popular with the Cree who traded them widely.

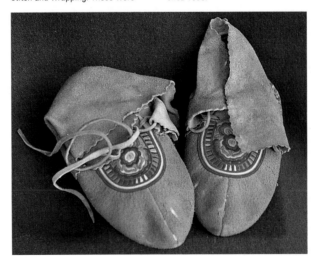

▼ A beautiful pair of Cree soft-soled, smoked moosehide moccasins decorated with a hard twist silk trade thread, using both a chain-stitch and wrapping. These were collected by a descendant of the early nineteenth century Hudson Bay official, Nicholas Garry, in the vicinity of Lake Winnipeg and date from *circa* 1880.

The future

Living in a land which does not lend itself to agriculture and where oil, gas and mining developments are prohibitively expensive, the Subarctic people are now facing a crisis. Their traditional livelihood of hunting and trapping is being opposed by anti-killing campaigns. What is not fully appreciated is that trapping is a source of income and that it both supports and perpetuates the Native American way of life in today's world. It is vital that this culture has an economic base and it is the fur trade which links the use of animals for subsistence with today's highly commercial economy. The Cree:

ᒥᕁᕐᑫᐧᓄᐊᐧᐃᐧᐲᐟ ᕁᑎᓯᐊ ᐊᐧᒪ ᓄ ᐃᐅᐲᐦᐲᐟ ᕁᑎᓯᐊ

which translates to 'Trapline, Lifeline', is a reference to their claim that they have a fundamental right to live according to the principles and skills inherent in their own traditional knowledge. It draws attention to the significance and value of hunting and trapping as a way of life, as well as the unquestionable right of an indigenous people to run their own affairs. In protecting their inherited knowledge in this way the Cree can continue to provide a foundation to their way of life, while at the same time maintaining a balanced standard of living. It remains to be seen how these resilient and resourceful people resolve this difficult dilemma.

ARCTIC: LIFE IN A LAND OF SNOW AND ICE

A study of human ingenuity

The Arctic cultural area extends more than three thousand miles (4,828km) from the Aleutian Islands in the Pacific Ocean east to include northern Quebec and the coast of Labrador. Whilst often depicted as a harsh and hostile land largely of snow and ice, in reality it is a region with several distinctive ecological zones and has an extensive coastline with major river systems into the interior.

Great expanses of tundra north of the tree line provide rich feeding grounds for musk-ox, caribou and wildfowl, whilst the rivers, their deltas and the sea are home to a wide variety of fish, as well as seals, walrus and whales. In the nineteenth century and earlier, the coastal waters abounded with sea-lions, sea-otters and fur seals.

One overriding characteristic of the Arctic region is the very limited amount of solar energy and, particularly north of the Arctic Circle, annual periods of continuous daylight or darkness. In July the average temperature over much of the region is 10°C (50°F), whilst in January it can drop to below -30°C (-22°F). With short, cool summers and long, cold winters, most of the subsoil remains frozen – a feature which is sometimes used to define the southern limit of the Arctic region.

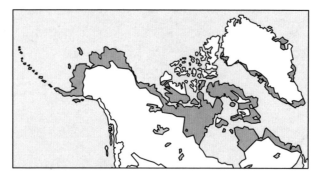

The Eskimo-Aleut cultural area extends for more than three thousand miles east to west and two thousand north to south, as far as the Gulf of St. Lawrence.

◀ Bering Strait Inuit woman and children, photographed about 1890. These people occupied almost twenty six thousand square miles (67,340 sq km), adjacent to the Bering Sea in western Alaska. Their population in the second half of the nineteenth century probably never exceeded two and a half thousand. Both woman and children are of a typical Eskimo type with long heads, short faces and well-marked Mongolian eyefolds.

The Eskimo people

The region is occupied by three major linguistic groups, the Aleut and Yupik west of the Beaufort Sea, and the Inuit-Inupiaq farther east extending to the Labrador Coast. All three groups probably descended from a predominately Eskimo-Aleut linguistic family who migrated from Asia across the Bering Strait some eight to ten thousand years ago. These people skillfully exploited the natural resources of their region sustaining a remarkably productive life, more often than not under the most adverse conditions.

Although commonly referred to as Eskimos, it is not a term popular with the people themselves, being derived from an Algonquian word which means 'raw meat eaters'. True, the Eskimo were not reluctant to eat raw offal, which provided them with essential nutrients for good health, so the term was sometimes appropriate. Indeed, the Eskimo were not unique, raw liver was considered a delicacy well south of the Arctic. As a result, the indigenous Arctic people have now elected to call themselves Inuit, regardless of any varying local usages. This translates to 'person' or 'people': 'the human beings' perhaps best conveys its full meaning.

Adaptation – the key to survival

Seal and caribou were the main staples of the Arctic people and everywhere man was a hunter, scant use being made of vegetable resources. Only the inland Caribou Inuit, devoid of sea mammal resources and dependent upon often erratic herd movements, ever lived with a real threat of famine.

Both physically and mentally, the Eskimo were well adapted to their environment. Of short stature and stocky build, bodily heat loss was minimal, whilst temperamentally they were long suffering, resourceful and skillful in all endeavours and good humoured. Anthropologists describe the Eskimo personality as pivoting on a 'Spartan ethic' where an individual was expected to develop and display such qualities as self-discipline and competence – both mentally and physically – in all spheres of activity demanded by the harsh Arctic environment in which he lived.

Among the Eskimo social and governmental organization was minimal. Some outstanding individuals did, however, wield considerable influence but if they exhibited tyrannical behaviour, they were likely to brought down by common consent – generally by their family, so avoiding any obligations of blood revenge. The essential unit was the extended family and full co-operation was a key component in communal hunting or indeed at any time of crisis. It was

A Pacific Eskimo settlement photographed about 1900. The women are sitting outside the typical turf- and straw-covered roof of their semi-subterranean home. Several families, up to twenty people, lived in such houses. Inside, was a main or common room off which were several floored, side chambers used for sleeping and privacy. The structure to the left was used for storage.

advantageous for an individual to marry outside his immediate group, so enlarging the web of family support. Marriage, as well as divorce, was largely devoid of ceremony. Some men had several wives but it was not altogether uncommon for a close partnership to grow up between two men, one then sharing the other's wife. This arrangement existed without apparent emotional strain, although occasionally jealousies did arise which ended in murder, at times leading to enduring blood feuds.

The cornerstone of Eskimo religious life was a complex taboo system which reflected the complexities of stress and unpredictability in their daily lives. Special care had to be taken not to offend the animal spirits, products of land and sea were not to be mixed, strict observances were to be met prior to the hunt and, on occasions, certain foods avoided. Arctic mythology validated these actions by giving meaning and structure to the spirit world; to ignore these obligations could bring sickness or even death and, as some protection from these unknown forces, most individuals possessed personal amulets or charms which were hung on their person or within their dwelling.

Habitations

The igloo, so well known as an Eskimo habitation was, in reality, mainly used by the Central Arctic Eskimo (*see below*). More widespread was the *karmak*, a partially subterranean earth-covered dwelling. Generally stone paved, it was entered through a low, sloping passage which had several recesses which could be used for storage. The basic framework was made of driftwood and whale ribs, the domed roof being covered with a thick layer of turf. Small windows of translucent rawhide or gut were set in the walls, additional light entering through a smoke hole in the roof.

During the spring and summer months, a tent made of caribou or seal skins and referred to as a *tupik* was widely used; since camps lived a partially nomadic existence during these milder seasons, the *tupik* had the advantage of being transportable.

On occasions, this dwelling, packed over with snow and ice for insulation, was also used in the sedentary winter time.

In constructing habitations, certain taboos were often observed, suggesting some type of symbolic association between the house and the womb. Particular attention was given to the final building step; in the case of the igloo, for example, it was said that the keystone had to be as large as possible

The igloo

The term 'igloo' is derived from the Inuit-Inupiaq word *igdlu*, which refers to a habitation where large blocks of snow and ice were used both as a structural support and covering. The type of snow and ice needed to be carefully selected; if too hard, it could not be cut, even with a trade metal knife which superseded that of antler or bone, yet on the other hand if the ice was too soft, the lower blocks crushed as the hemisphere was built. It took two skilled men several hours to complete the basic structure, the snow blocks being built up in a spiral fashion, gradually leaning inwards until the roof was closed in. A tunnel-like entrance was also built by the men and during this time the less-skilled women and children filled in the small holes and slits between the blocks with snow. Care was taken to ensure that a small air hole was left in the roof and light was let into the igloo by means of a sheet of clear ice set into the wall above the entrance tunnel.

A platform of ice generally ran around the interior of the igloo; covered with skins and mats it served as both bench and bed. Whilst an average igloo could house up to six or seven people, it was not infrequently added to with smaller igloos for use by elderly parents, a young married couple or simply for storage of food and equipment – all linked together by carefully constructed tunnels.

An essential device in such dwellings was a small stone lamp fuelled by seal or blubber oil and having a wick of moss or grass. Carefully attended by the senior women in the family, it provided not only warmth and light, but was also used to cook and dry clothing. The interior of the igloo frequently reached a constant temperature of 30°C (86°F) and men, women and children generally discarded outer clothing and boots on entering, moving about the igloo barefoot and wearing only trousers. Travellers could put up a small overnight igloo in less than an hour, but large igloos for communal ceremonies took several days.

▲ Copper Inuit building an igloo, photographed about 1915. Such dwellings were used from early winter until late spring.

▲ North Alaska Coast Eskimo summer settlement, photographed about 1900. This region falls mainly north of the Arctic Circle where whaling was a hallmark of the indigenous culture. Both domed and conically-shaped structures, probably covered with caribou hides, are shown here, as are frames for drying meat and fish (*left background, right foreground*) and huskies resting near the winter sleds (*left foreground*).

to ensure easy childbirth for the mothers. When completed, the Eskimo habitation was considered to be a microcosm of the outside world. Thus, the floor area in the igloo was viewed as associated with men, the accoutrements which they used and the seas in which they hunted. Sitting and sleeping platforms, on the other hand, were associated with women as was the warmth and light which was provided by the oil lamps.

▼ An *ulu* knife with the typical half-moon iron blade and T-shaped metal grip. These knives were used for a variety of purposes, such as skinning and cutting meat and hides. A cleverly designed and versatile tool, it is now to be found in many modern North American kitchens.

Arts and craft

Whatever the style of dwelling, the interior generally presented a lively, busy scene, women spending much of their time repairing and making clothing and cooking food – traditionally in pots of carved soapstone. Men busied themselves making and repairing hunting equipment, carving musk-ox horn and soapstone utensils and producing ornaments of wood, ivory and bone, many of striking originality, distinctively Eskimo and frequently in miniature.

One most essential tool of Eskimo women was the ulu, a knife with a crescent-shaped blade and a bone or wooden handle. It was used not only for cutting meat and skinning animals but also for making clothing (of such clever design and versatility, it is now commonly found in the modern North American kitchen!).

Warm clothing was essential for permanent residence above the tree line and the fundamental principles of thermal insulation were well understood. Most of the clothing worn was two-layered, with the inner fur side in and outer fur side out, a layer of quiescent air thus being trapped between the two skin surfaces. A combination of seal and caribou skin was generally used producing shirts, trousers and boots which were so cleverly and carefully sewn with sinew thread from the narwhal whale that the seams were waterproof.

Hooded shirts, commonly referred to as *parkas*, were widely used. Whilst there were considerable regional variations in style of this popular garment, universally the hood was adapted for carrying babies.

In the damp, wet climate of the Aleutian Islands, waterproof garments were of paramount importance. Thus, seal intestines dried and cut into strips were pieced together, the seams embellished with coloured hair or tufts of coloured thread or wool. Thin strips of dyed rawhide, generally stitched on with caribou hair and worked in delicate, intricate patterns, added to the decoration. Shirts, trousers, boots and hats were all produced using the versatile, almost translucent, gut material. Whilst on the Aleutian Islands one form of head protection was a wooden peaked helmet, another style of head covering, somewhat resembling a Russian hat, but made of gut rather than wool, was very popular (*see top right*).

▲ A fine Aleut hat made of pieces of translucent seal intestine and decorated with dyed rawhide, wrapped hair and wool. These were commonly worn by *kayak* and *umiak* sea hunters and the style was possibly derived from the Russian sailor's hat.

◄ A Labrador Coast Eskimo model of a female figure dressed in a typical sealskin *parka* and wearing high skin boots typical of the region. Note the figure of a child in the hood of the *parka*. This model dates from about 1900 and was collected by the Rev. and Mrs. Callendar, missionaries from England.

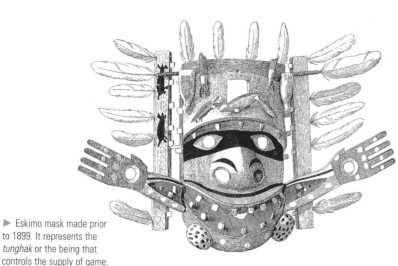

► Eskimo mask made prior to 1899. It represents the *tunghak* or the being that controls the supply of game. The figurines represent five seals and two caribou.

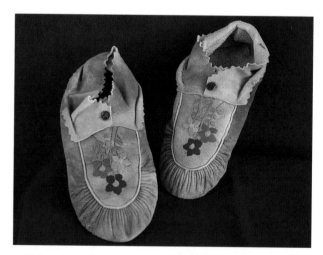

▲ During spring and summer, particularly where Eskimo and Subarctic culture overlapped, soft-soled, puckered moccasins were worn. These are made of smoked caribou hide embellished with coloured threads and were collected in Labrador about 1910.

The *parka*

Both caribou and sealskin, with the hair left on, were used in the construction of a shirt or gown which was worn in various forms by men, women and children throughout the Arctic region. Commonly referred to as a *parka*, both cut and mode of decoration distinguished between those used by men or women. Whilst obviously giving protection from the physical forces of nature, in the case of the man's *parka* it symbolically made reference to him as a hunter, while the woman's, displaying the characteristic pouch, symbolized her maternal role.

Complex patterns contrasting white, black and various shades of brown were achieved by use of

◄ North Alaskan Coast Inuits wearing *parkas* which were essential garments for the hostile Arctic environment. Note also the labrets, ornaments of ivory and bone, which were worn in holes pierced through the lips.

different parts of the caribou or seal's pelt. Many *parkas*, particularly in the early historic period, featured a long black tail which was said to make a metaphoric reference to animals and also to the Eskimo as a hunting culture. Generally the hood

of the woman's *parka* was fuller than that of the man's providing a pouch that could be used for carrying a baby who, with nappies of moss pads, not only shared the warmth of the mother's body, but also virtually the same viewpoint!

Transportation and the hunt

Unlike the Indian tribes of the Subarctic who used a flat-bottomed toboggan, the Eskimo employed a true sled pulled by dogs which had wooden side runners which were generally shod with bone (*see Inuit models and carvings, page 84*). Referred to as a *komatik*, it was lashed together with rawhide and sinew, the crosswise wooden slats carrying loads of up to 400 lb (180 kg).

The Arctic people, however, nowhere displayed their natural ingenuity more than in the design of the *kayak*. Although varying considerably in style from one region to the next, all were made of a frame of driftwood with bone or ivory used for reinforcement. The framework was covered with sealskin impregnated with oil both to waterproof and keep it flexible. Propelled by a narrow-bladed wooden paddle, with the occupant snugly fitted into the cockpit and hood and sleeves tightly closed by drawstrings, craft and man were virtually unsinkable. Mainly used for hunting, the *kayak* was a craft of outstanding speed and manoeuvrability. It carried on its deck, harpoons, stabbing spear or knife, sealskin buoys and special netted drags for attaching to the quarry. Some *kayaks* – the Aleutian type being referred to by early Russian traders as *baidarkas* – had two hatches considerably increasing effectiveness in landing the quarry after the initial strike.

► A Bering Strait Eskimo using an *atlatl* to throw a harpoon. All tribes in this region used the one-holed *kayak*, propelled by a double or single paddle, as shown here. Note the spare harpoons and the small buoy behind the figure. The buoy was used to keep the quarry, seal or walrus, afloat.

Larger crews were carried in the so-called *umiak*. Constructed of drift-wood and covered with walrus or seal hides and up to forty feet (12m) in length, they were used mainly in whaling. Unlike the *kayak*, the *umiak* had both sail and paddle propulsion, enabling hunting excursions well into the open seas in search of the enormous bowhead whale which could be up to seventy feet (21m) in length. Such a creature was an invaluable source of food, shelter, clothing and ornament – virtually nothing was wasted of the carcass by these resourceful, ingenious people.

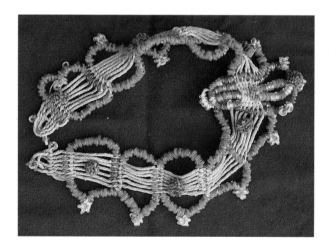

▲ A dog harness made of hemp and decorated with large trade beads and red and green wool tufts which would help locate the animal in deep snow. This rare item was collected from the Labrador Coast Eskimo about 1910.

Inuit models and carvings

Universally in the Arctic region, individuals made superb models of everyday items, such as *kayaks*, *umiaks* and other domestic and hunting equipment, and dolls. In addition, miniature sculptures were often produced to be used as a personal talisman or as an embellishment for hats and clothing. Although the models and sculptures, following ancient tradition, were used in the instruction and entertainment of children, they later became important items of trade, particularly to European sailors seeking exotic souvenirs.

Dolls, beautifully clothed down to the finest detail, served to instruct girls in the intricate techniques of sewing and patterning demanded in the proper embellishment and use of the *parka*, whilst models of

such important devices as the *komatik*, 'sled', taught boys the correct method of harnessing the dog and securing the heavy loads.

Wood, bone, soapstone and caribou antler were the most commonly used media but the most valuable raw material was ivory, from the walrus tooth. It was carved – although it required great patience

▲ A model skin *kayak* with human figure seated in the cockpit. This is a fine example of Eskimo craftsmanship in the miniature, showing *kayak* and paddles reinforced with bone and ivory and details of the *parka* laced round the face and wrists of the wearer.

and skill – with a flint (later iron) blade and then polished with soft stone or sand.

Finely carved and engraved amulets, which were considered to give personal protection, were invariably made of ivory, the time required to fabricate them fitting in well with the Eskimo ethic that superior craftsmanship was pleasing to the spirits. Carefully carved cases of ivory were used for storing needles and pins.

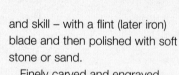

▼ A Labrador Eskimo model, carved from bone, of a sled pulled by huskies.

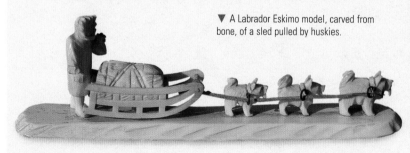

INDIANS IN THE TWENTIETH CENTURY

Wounded Knee – 29 December, 1890 – saw the final closing of the frontier, the indigenous inhabitants of a vast and rich continent were now finally confined to reservations and reserves throughout the United States and Canada: the colonization of North America by Euro-Americans was complete, all that remained for The People were their memories.

▲ The mass grave at Wounded Knee cemetery in South Dakota. On a cold December day in 1890, a human tragedy occurred which has never been forgotten or lost its poignancy. Although it directly impacted on the Miniconjou Sioux under their chief, Big Foot – almost two hundred men, women and children of his band died – it has become a symbol for American Indians in general, the last stand of North America's indigenous people in the nineteenth century.

Iron Tail or *Sinte Maza* – a bridge between cultures

Iron Tail, or *Sinte Maza*, was an Oglala Sioux born in a buffalo hide tipi in Dakota Territory in 1847. He became a warrior and fine horseman and, it is said, fought in the Custer Battle of 25 June, 1876.

When Buffalo Bill formed his Wild West Show in 1883, he engaged a number of famous old Indians, among them Iron Tail who stayed and travelled with Buffalo Bill's Shows through all their tours.

Iron Tail was considered a very fine Indian, always smiling and very fond of jokes upon himself and others. He became a valued companion and friend of Buffalo Bill who, more than once, considered him a sufficient star attraction to advertise The Show by means of lavish coloured posters showing a portrait of Iron Tail resplendent in a feathered warbonnet.

In 1913, another honour was bestowed on Iron Tail when James Earle Fraser chose him as one of his subjects to model for the Indian

▲ Iron Tail, Sinte Maza, an Oglala Sioux who travelled with Buffalo Bill's Shows and became a valued companion and friend of Buffalo Bill.

head that appears on the famous buffalo nickel. *Sinte Maza*, it should also be emphasized, was not only distinguished as an entertainer, he also took a keen interest in his tribe's history, providing information for scholarly researchers. Foremost,

however, he was an image maker, invariably appearing in beaded buckskin regalia and wearing a magnificent eagle-feathered warbonnet. This image came to epitomize that of the American Indian and has been perpetuated throughout the twentieth century not only by Whites, but also by North American Indians, as widely separated as from Nova Scotia to Gallup, New Mexico.

Iron Tail died in May 1916 and is buried at the Holy Rosary Mission on the Pine Ridge Reservation in South Dakota close to another famous Oglala Sioux, *Makhpiya-lúta* 'Red Cloud'.

Although, as we move towards the millennium, the perception and image of the American Indian is constantly changing, the world owes much to the likes of Iron Tail for he helped to bridge the gap between alien cultures and with dignity and honour projected the best of his people.

To alleviate the boredom of reservation life and to earn money to survive, many former warriors – sometimes also their wives and children – moved into the business of entertainment, joining such companies as Buffalo Bill's Wild West Show. This show, which first opened with great success in Omaha, Nebraska in May 1883, re-enacted exciting episodes in the history of the Old West and travelled widely throughout America and Europe.

Buffalo Bill's Wild West Show was a major attraction at Queen Victoria's Golden Jubilee celebrations in England in 1877, playing to enormous audiences of up to forty thousand, (sadly, some of the Indians in that show never returned home). Such spectacular entertainment served to preserve the Plains Indian as a symbol of the North American Indian, an image of everything that was 'Indian'. The eagle-feathered, war-bonneted warrior was copied and perpetuated by tribes as widely spaced as the Micmac of Nova Scotia, the Pueblo of New Mexico and the Cherokee in North Carolina. Thirty years later, Iron Eyes Cody – of Cree and Cherokee descent – made his name in another branch of the entertainment business, the Hollywood movie. He became 'probably the most famous American Indian actor' appearing in over two hundred films and crowning his career with a meeting with the Pope, remarking 'Of all the world leaders I've met, he was the warmest, the most human'.

For more than a generation the suppressed Indians on the reservations, whose traditional way of life had been totally destroyed, struggled to survive. Some, such as the Mohawk, realizing the futility of further opposition, turned to creating a New America and trained as steelworkers. Mohawks were active in erecting such bridges as the Sault Sainte Marie Bridge in northern Michigan and the Quebec Bridge across the St. Lawrence. Later, they were involved in the erection of the huge buildings in New York, including the Empire State Building. Today, a new generation of Mohawks and other Iroquois continue the tradition and are willing to travel to virtually anywhere in the

▶ The Oglala, Long Wolf, who travelled with his family to London, England in 1892 as a member of Buffalo Bill's Wild West Show. Sadly, he developed bronchial pneumonia whilst staying with the Show at the Earl's Court Exhibition Ground and died in June 1892, at the age of 59, in the West London Hospital. He is buried in Brompton Cemetery and the cross above his grave bears the fading carved outline of a wolf's head. His descendents are hoping to transfer his remains back to his homeland on Pine Ridge Reservation, South Dakota.

▲ Many Mohawks trained as high steel workers, distinguishing themselves in the trade. They helped erect bridges such as the Sault Sainte Marie in northern Michigan, the Quebec Bridge across the St. Lawrence and, later, most of New York's skyscrapers. But it was dangerous work, incurring amongst the largest number of accidents in the construction industry, killing and permanently injuring many of them. The large iron cross, with the image of Christ crucified, on the main altar in the church at St. Francis Xavier Mission, Kahnawake, Quebec commemorates the loss of thirty-five Mohawks from Kahnawake who died when the partially completed Quebec Bridge collapsed in August 1907. This tragedy is still spoken of as 'the disaster'.

United States or Canada to find both jobs and new adventures. The work, however, was done at great cost as many Iroquois have died or been permanently injured over the years.

Throughout most of the reservations there was despair and great dissatisfaction, entire tribes – indeed whole cultural areas – falling into a state where all the old values no longer held any meaning and the conditions necessary for self-fulfilment and the attainment of happiness ceased to exist. The situation was aggravated by the complexities of American democracy, differing and opposing departmental interests, shifting political power, the limited authority of individuals – difficulties faced by a new nation, finding its way.

The passing of the Indian Reorganization Act in 1934 by President Roosevelt saw a shift in attitudes. This provided for a degree of tribal self-government and made funds available to develop schools, hospitals and cultural amenities. It represented the beginning of a series of government initiatives to improve the material quality of life of American Indians which reached its height during the Kennedy and Johnson administrations.

Today American Indians, now proud of a culture which almost died, travel widely explaining to increasingly appreciative audiences the ethos of their people, although they face a new revolution – the possible end of the reservation system.

The Crow Fair

From the early 1900s the third weekend in August has seen the start of the Crow Fair on the Little Bighorn River in south-central Montana. The location is near the battlefield where George Armstrong Custer, together with two hundred and twenty-five officers and men, made a last stand against the joint forces of Sioux and Cheyenne under the spiritual leadership of *Tatan'ha-iyo'take*, 'Sitting Bull'.

This has been the traditional Crow meeting ground since the late nineteenth century. Each year the largest collection of tipis in the world is pitched here, clusterering around a dance circle. Indians from all over North America, and other visitors, are hosted for an important time of gathering and powwowing.

In buffalo-hunting days, the Crow were famous for their white, tanned tipi covers, and the great lodge poles which gave the tipi its hourglass look. Today the covers are made of canvas.

There are almost daily parades, providing an opportunity to display new types of regalia and equipment and whilst horses predominate, trucks and cars are often decorated with beaded clothing and feathered headdresses. Traditional costume is worn, the women wearing elk teeth dresses, the men in warbonnets and beaded shirts and leggings.

Crow Fair is a place to visit to see much of the traditional life and times of the old-time Plains Indians.

▲ A Crow girl on horseback wearing traditional costume, decorated with elk teeth. The horse regalia is of fine beadwork in typical Crow style.

◀ Sarah Spotted Elk and grandchildren, Fort Yates, North Dakota, photographed in 1966. The family lived on the reservation in a log cabin, with no running water. Mrs Spotted Elk's husband was dying of leukaemia but she had much time for her beloved grandchildren and made traditional costumes for them embellished with dentalium shells and beadwork.

American Indian artists

The Native Americans, as the previous chapters have shown, produced a huge variety of art forms – petroglyphs, pictographs, carvings in wood, bone, horn and stone – in the prehistoric and historic times. This trend continues today, a recent survey identifying almost two hundred Native American artists from different regions of North America (*American Indian Art* magazine, Winter, 1995). These artists work in a variety of media, some very traditional, such as carvers in pipestone (*see below*), others experiment with less traditional materials, such as alabaster, welded steel and the opaque watercolour medium gouache; most of it is highly innovative and stunningly imaginative.

Many of these individuals were (and still are) teachers, as though the notion of sharing their expertise as well as their culture was, in fact, an important part of their heritage.

Indian art in stone – a continuing tradition

Today, the Pipestone Quarry in Minnesota is designated as a National Monument. Here a number of Chippewa and Sioux craftsmen, many of third or fourth generation pipe-makers, carry on the art. In addition to the wide variety of pipes made by the resident Indian craftsmen, others have extended their skills to produce more practical objects, often incorporating highly imaginative ideas.

▲ Continuing traditions – Northwest Coast cultural heritage. Members of the family of Norman Tait, a distinguished Northwest Coast Nishga artist (the Nishga are a tribe of the Tsimshian of northwestern British Columbia and with the Tlingit and Haida, renowned for their wood carving).

The scene shows an episode at the time of erection of an Eagle Killer Whale Pole (carved by Norman Tait), in Bushy Park, London, on the occasion of the 1992 Canada Day. Note the traditional button blankets with the family crests and the carved eagle which was attached to the top of the pole.

▼ The *Wiwanyang Wacipi*, 'gaze at the sun' or Sun Dance (*see also page 17*), Pine Ridge Reservation, August 1966. With the new wave of pride in cultural heritage and the relaxation of white officials towards traditional Sioux religion, the first piercing for more than eighty years took place at Pine Ridge in 1966. Shown here is the central Sun Dance pole and the dancers, each pierced and attached by a cord from their chests to the pole and blowing on a whistle made of eagle bone.

One outstanding artist whose media extended from marble to limestone, alabaster, slate, bronze, steel and wood, was Allan Houser (1914–94). Of Chiricahua Apache and English descent, his father, Samuel Haozous was a member of Geronimo's band of Apache resistance fighters. Allan Houser trained as a muralist but in the 1940s he began to turn his attention to sculpture. Towards the end of his life, Houser put great emphasis on human dignity in his sculptures, stating 'this is what I strive for – this dignity, this goodness that is man'.

◀ Looking Eagle, a noted Sioux craftsman, *circa* 1964. He and his Chippewa wife, Winona, worked at the Pipestone Quarry in Minnesota for many years producing traditional style pipes from the coveted catlinite. He is shown here working on a pipe blank, rounding the shank and bowl with a file; he will then give it a high-polish finish.

The Studio at Santa Fe Indian School

Founded in September 1932 by Dorothy Dunn, a Chicago Art Institute graduate with a great interest in Indian art, The Studio at the Santa Fe Indian School, as it came to be known, received official recognition in 1933 from the Federal Government as a centre for study of American Indian painters.

Numerous Indian artists from all parts of the United States and Canada went through The Studio, including Wilmer Dupree (much influenced by the earlier Sioux historian, Amos Bad Heart Bull), Ernie Farmer, a Bannock-Shoshone, and Victor Pepion, Blackfeet – the latter two being cited for honours at The Studio. These, and many others, subsequently went on as teachers to create both traditional and innovative works of art relating to the American Indian scene.

One of the most outstanding students at the Santa Fe School, was the Yanktonai Dakota, *Mazuha Hokshina* or 'Trader Boy' (1915–83) who entered in 1935 and graduated as a salutatorian in 1938. He later went on to inspire and give confidence to many younger American Indian artists, such as Robert Penn, Arthur Amiotte and Laurie Houseman-Whitehawk, who are all still active in the field. Penn's series of paintings relating to the plight of the Urban Indian is, in his own estimation, the most telling theme of his artistic career, both personally and artistically.

Oscar Howe: the father of the new Native American art

Oscar Howe – *Mazuha Hokshina* or 'Trader Boy' – was a Yanktonai Sioux born on the Crow Creek Indian Reservation in 1915. His family line included a number of hereditary chiefs, several of whom represented their tribe during the turbulent years of Indian-White confrontation, particularly in the last quarter of the nineteenth century. As one biographer of Oscar Howe – Professor John A. Day – has observed, 'his personal history was as trying as that of his people; a paradigm of their travail and definitely a symbol of their perseverance'.

Sent to a Bureau of Indian Affairs boarding school at the age of seven where he was subjected to a harsh system which was, at that time, committed to the assimilation of the Indian, he left ill and demoralized. He eventually returned to the reservation where under the kindly care of his grandmother, Shell Face, he learnt the richness of his Sioux heritage which was to have a profound effect on his life's work. Showing a natural ability in art, in 1935, with the aid of a government grant, he was given the opportunity

to develop this talent professionally, joining The Studio at the Indian School in Santa Fe, run by the artist Dorothy Dunn. After graduation, he continued to develop his style which was strongly influenced by his Sioux heritage, emerging in the 1960s between stylized abstractions and non-objective interpretations.

Mazuha Hokshina's work was deeply embedded in Sioux culture – rituals, ceremonials, myths and occasionally tribal history: his abstractions enhanced the impact of the art work he produced having, as John Day has observed, 'dynamic energy, poetic presence and sense of reverence'.

The artist, *Wicanpe* or 'Star', better known as Robert Penn (*right*) with the author, photographed in 1995 at his home near the Vermillion River in South Dakota. Robert Penn's parents were Omaha and Rosebud Sioux. He himself studied (1966–72) under the renowned Sioux artist, Oscar Howe (*see page 89*) who greatly encouraged his work. One of the themes in Penn's work has been the problem of America's urban Indians and the difficulties which they face in white society.

Urban Indian by *Wicanpe*, Robert Penn. Drawing attention to the problems of Indians when they attempt to move to cities has been the central theme of Penn's work and is one which, in his own estimation, has been the most telling of his artistic career.

Charcoal sketch of the noted Blackfeet, Big-Bull, produced by the Blackfeet artist, Gerald Tailfeathers (1925–75) who was known at school as 'the genius'. His Blackfeet name was *Its-Papa-Wachka*, meaning 'Walking-On-Top'. The artist and author, Clare Sheridan – who bought this drawing from Gerald Tailfeathers himself in 1938 for five dollars – described him as 'an artist, as truly as anyone can be'. Here Big-Bull wears a Sioux style warbonnet, adopted by the Blackfeet (as a sign of 'Indianness'), in the late nineteenth century.

American Indian Scholars

For over two hundred years, American Indian authors have published their written work, reaching an appreciative, largely white, audience. In 1772 the Mohegan, Samson Occom, published *Sermon Preached on the Execution of Moses Paul*, which despite its morbid theme, became the first Indian best-seller. Over a century later, another popular Indian author, the Sioux, *Ohiyesa*, Charles Eastman, published various books on American Indian life, perhaps his most moving being *Soul of the Indian* (1911) in which he described the worship of the 'Great Mystery'. Later, in *The Indian Today* (1915), Eastman made a significant survey of Indian history, their achievements and contribution to America, reservation life and Indian problems.

By the 1930s increasing numbers of American Indians emerged as accomplished and prolific writers. For example the Osage, John Joseph Mathews, and the Cree/Salish, D'Arcy McNickle, who both emphasized the importance of maintaining tribal integrity and drew attention to the government's assimilation policies which had a devastating impact on the tribes.

The revitalization of American Indian pride in the 1960s led to an era of high-quality writing, such as that of the Pulitzer prize winner, N. Scott Momaday (Kiowa) who stressed the problems of Indians in contemporary society, the importance of oral ritual and tradition and the use of memory to structure plot. Later, in the 1970s and 1980s, came Gerald Vizenor (Ojibwa) a 'masterful writer of non-fiction prose' who perceptively portrays the wounds suffered by Indians as a result of the clash between the white and tribal worlds. This clash is vividly underlined by the Oto/Pawnee, Anna Walter's novel, *Ghost Singer* (1988), which focuses on Navajo-White relations and the Whites' practice of storing Indian skeletons, body parts, and sacred possessions in museums – issues which are at the forefront of the repatriation scheme launched by the National Museum of the American Indian.

A Powhatan village on the Virginia tidewater

One of the most interesting interpretative sites, of a powerful and highly influential tribe, is that of a reconstructed village of the Powhatan Indians whose territory at the time of the establishment of the first English colony at Jamestown in 1607, extended across most of present-day Virginia and northern North Carolina. At that time the great chief, *Powhatan*, together with his three brothers, *Opechancanough*, *Optitchapan* and *Kecatough*, had formed a Confederacy which united at least twenty-eight tribes and occupied more than one hundred and sixty villages.

A typical Powhatan village was a semi-permanent site, the larger villages included up to one hundred wigwams with a surrounding palisade, a temple, storehouses and a dance circle used for religious and social ceremonials. In the vicinity were fields and gardens where various varieties of corn, together with peas, beans, sunflowers, pumpkins and tobacco, were grown. The surrounding forests provided a variety of fruits, nuts and roots, the rivers and estuaries an

John White's sketch of Secota village (*left*). The dance circle with carved posts (*above* and *below*) is in the bottom right hand corner of the sketch, the hut for the watchman guarding against birds is top right.

abundance of fish, such as sturgeon and herring. There was no shortage of meat – deer, bear, squirrel, rabbit, turkey, ducks and geese.

The village of Secota was drawn by the English artist, John White, one of Sir Walter Raleigh's colonists who visited Virginia in the late sixteenth century. In his sketch, he shows burial sites of the chiefs, areas where the tribe assembled to pray and celebrate feasts, the gardens – even the hut used by the watchman to guard against the birds eating the ripe corn. Most of these scenes have been reconstructed at the village site, giving a glimpse of a rich culture which flourished more than four hundred years ago.

Education

The soujourn, in 1841 of *Oronhyatekha*, a Mohawk born on the Six Nations Reserve, near Brantford, Ontario, at St. Edmund Hall, a college of the University of Oxford in England, underlined the ability of an American Indian to make his own way in the white man's world. *Oronhyatekha* went on to qualify as a medical doctor who practiced in the Ontario communities.

Clearly, a white man's education suited this enterprising Mohawk scholar in the nineteenth century. One hundred years later, however, the white man's approach to education has been firmly rejected by the Navajo, a recent report on a bid to overcome Native American suspicion of schooling, suggesting that western education formats do not get results in reservation schools. Addressing such problems was the theme of a recent convention of the National Indian Education Association held at the Rushmore Plaza Civic Center in October 1996. Titled as *Wounspe Wopika*, 'Education at its best', and hosted by the 'Great Sioux Nation', they have evolved an educational philosophy which aims to provide innovative and creative ways of teaching Indian children, promoting tribal cultures and traditions. Associated activities were powwows, one of which included a buffalo feed.

Following in the footsteps of *Oronhyatekha*, were many others, such as D'Arcy McNickle and, more recently, Dr. Barbara Feezor-Stewart, an enrolled Yankton Sioux and visiting assistant professor at the Arizona State University in Phoenix, and Scott Bear Don't Walk, a registered member of the Crow tribe who, in 1992, won a Rhodes Scholarship to Merton College, Oxford, England. A philosophy major, Bear Don't Walk wants to use his experience to help bridge the gap between American Indians and Whites.

▲ Scott Bear Don't Walk who is a registered member of the Crow, confederated Salish and Kootenai tribes and was a Rhodes Scholar to Merton College, Oxford, England in 1992. He is a traditionalist as well as a modernist! A philosophy major, he was one of thirty-two students selected from thirteen hundred applicants. Scott Bear Don't Walk said he viewed the scholarship 'as a chance for some of the people who have experienced colonization … to sort of get back what was taken'.

▲ Barbara Feezor-Stewart, an enrolled Yankton Sioux and a blood relative of the Minnesota Mdewakanton Dakota. An eminent academic, she has won numerous awards for professional service and academic excellence. She trained in Western European traditions at the University of California, Berkeley, receiving a Ph.D in anthropology in 1994. She is now (1996) an assistant professor in the American Studies Department at Arizona State University in Phoenix.

The wampum belts go back home

The Iroquois referred to wampum belts as *Kari hwa*, the 'authentic credential', or *gawenna*, 'the voice, the word, the proposition', and they played a key role in the governing process of the Iroquoian Confederacy. They were used to seal all treaties, agreements or pledges. The motifs worked on them symbolized important events, the significance of which the Keepers of the wampum were responsible for remembering.

In 1893, Chief *Skananktis*, Keeper of the wampum belts for the Six Nations, died at which time at least eleven belts went missing. These found their way to the Museum of the American Indian, Heye Foundation, New York, where they resided for more than two generations.

In 1898, four of the belts, Hiawatha, Washington Covenant, First Pale Faces and Champlain, which commemorate major events in the history of the Iroquois Confederacy and the United States, were transferred by the Onondaga chiefs to the University of the State of New York. In 1988, eleven belts were returned to the Six Nations Reserve and in 1989 chiefs of the Onondaga Nation and representatives of the University, signed a document to return twelve of the belts (created between 1650 and 1800) to the Iroquois people.

◀ The return of the Haiwatha belt in 1989. *From left to right:* Onondaga Chief Irving Powless, former Chief Leon Shenandoah (who died in 1996) and Dr. Martin Sullivan, then Director, New York State Museum, Albany.

Echoes of the past; voices of the future

The current interest in the ancient Americas, has led to the development of a large number of sites important to the history of the American Indian. Battlefields, forts, ancient village and hunting sites are all being reconstructed, reinterpreted and, in some cases often due to recommendations by the Indian people themselves, renamed – such as the Custer Battlefield – which, in December 1991, was renamed the Little Bighorn Battlefield National Monument. Likewise with tribal designations, many tribes now describing themselves as 'Nations'. A major initiative approved by Congress and signed into law by President Bush on 28 November, 1989, was the launching of the National Museum of the American Indian, with the intention of inspiring an exponential increase in Native American studies with a range of new ideas for exhibitions, research and insight into historic and contemporary Indian culture. A major concern of the new museum was to formulate a repatriation policy of not only American Indian human remains, but also funerary objects, communally-owned Native property, ceremonial and religious objects and objects transferred to or acquired by the museum illegally to Indian tribes or individuals with tribal or cultural affiliation. Religious and ceremonial objects are now to be exhibited only with the approval of the relevant tribe.

Problems of identification, however, are arising, particularly amongst groups east of the Missouri-Mississippi where Indian blood has been diluted by intermarriage. It is now viewed as advantageous on several counts to have Indian blood and many people are coming forward claiming an American Indian heritage. But, as one Mohegan involved in the lucrative casino enterprises has said, 'you can't just turn up and say 200 years ago I had a Mohican great-great-great-great-grandfather. You don't become tribal overnight. Only people who can prove a continuous social and political contact are admitted to the tribe'. Sentiments echoed by many tribal councils whose concern for rebuilding their shattered culture is of paramount importance – the term 'plastic Indian' is taking on a new meaning!

▲ Model of the proposed National Museum of the American Indian building, showing the north side which faces the National Mall in Washington D.C. The principal designer of this building is the Blackfeet Indian, Douglas Cardinal, who now lives in Ottawa, Ontario.

The director of this new museum is W. Richard West, a trained attorney and member of the Cheyenne-Arapaho tribes of Oklahoma. The construction of this six-floor building is scheduled to commence in 1998 and the public opening is planned for the year 2002.

Indian Casinos: life beyond government dependency?

The biggest cuts in the Federal budget forced through Congress in 1995–6 related to the funding which enabled tribes to administer their own education, housing, economic development and police services. This is a governmental initiative to end the dependency culture of the reservations, which has been in place for more than a century.

The measure of sovereignty which American Indians have over their tribal lands, including the right to be spared the state taxes, has, since American Indian gaming started in the early 1980s, been put to good use in an effort to offset the loss of Government revenue.

In 1995, over two hundred Indian-owned casinos were established, producing almost $3 billion in profits. Not all, however, are benefiting; of the five hundred and fifty-five Federally recognized tribes, it is estimated that no more than twenty-five have any significant income from the casinos.

Amongst the most successful of the Indian casinos, is the vast one run by the Mashantucket Pequot of Connecticut, at Foxwoods (*above*), close to New York City, which takes

an estimated $600 million a year. The tiny Pequot Reservation on which no more than three hundred and eighty registered tribes-people live, has been likened to the equivalent of America's Brunei and the tribe has been able to construct for itself a socialist worker's paradise. Millions of dollars have been ploughed into education, health and welfare, as well as substantial investments made off the reservation, even in a company on the Isle of Wight, England who are building high speed ferries! Tradition is not forgotten however and regular powwows are held at Foxwoods.

America's third largest casino, near the Connecticut port of New London, belongs to the Mohegan. With an investment of $285 million, the eleven hundred surviving tribe members are poised to enter a new world of growth and prosperity.

Huge profits may not last – the Republicans have already approved legislation imposing an extraordinary 34% tax on the profits of all Indian-run casinos. As Buzz Two Lance, an Oglala Sioux who runs the Indian Radio Station on the Pine Ridge Reservation observed, 'as soon as the white man sees the Indians with a good thing, he takes it'!

INDEX

NOTES ON THE MOTIFS

These are all from North American Indian pictographs and petroglyphs or weavings of various sorts, dating from the period approximately 1800–1900. Interpretation of many of these has not always been recorded; they are, however, typical of a particular culture area.

Talking Wall (page 6) *Clockwise from top right:*

1 Running buffalo. Note the careful delineation of the hooves. Cheyenne (Great Plains), *circa* 1880. The flow of action is clearly indicated by the extended legs.
2 A Texas bull. Lone Dog's winter count (Sioux, Plains), documenting the introduction of the 'spotted buffalo' into Dakota Territory in 1868–69.
3 Rider on horseback. A motif based on a Northern Plains Indian petroglyph. Note the large shield – a style inherited from earlier pedestrian warfare. The peculiar 'hook' features at the end of the horse's legs are hoof prints, commonly used to identify the horse in Plains petroglyphs/pictographs.
4 Rendering of a bear. Pictograph by a Tanaina (Subarctic) artist, *circa* 1840.
5 Sun-burst design. Such large scale motifs were used on buffalo robes and were said to represent the warbonnet; they were particularly favoured by the Mandan and Hidatsa (Plains) and usually date prior to 1850.
6 Warrior with gun. Drawn by a Crow (Plains) artist, *circa* 1850. Probably a Pawnee – note the distinctive hair-lock.
7 Rendering of a beaver. Tanaina (Subarctic), *circa* 1840. Note the distinctive flat tail; these creatures were an important source of fur and food to the Subarctic tribes.
8 Diamond-shaped figures enclosing a rectangle, from a Nez Perce (Plateau) bag, *circa* 1880. Such designs were commonly used by this tribe and they also appear as paintings on rawhide.
9 Mountain sheep showing the characteristic large horns. Pictograph on buckskin. Tanaina (Subarctic), *circa* 1840.

Introduction (page 7) *Clockwise from top right:*

1 Caribou hunter. Tanaina Indian (Subarctic), dating from *circa* 1840.
2 Warrior carrying bow and musket. Mandan (Great Plains), dating from *circa* 1800. This is typical of the style of pictograph showing a human figure for this early period.
3 A conventionalized Thunderbird(?) design. Nez Perce (Plateau), dating from *circa* 1880. Taken from a Nez Perce woven cornhusk bag, for which the tribe was famous.
4 Warrior showing breechcloth and distinctive hair-style. Crow (Great Plains), a typical pictograph of a man from *circa* 1870.
5 Figure of a man. Oto (Prairie), possibly using a gesture sign for peace.
6 Tipi decorated with buffalo head. Sans Arc (Teton Sioux sub-tribe, Great Plains). Used when Sans Arc performed buffalo-calling ceremonials in the winter of 1843–44. The pictograph, by *Sun'ka-ishnala*, 'Lone Dog', dates from *circa* 1875.
7 Design from a cornhusk wallet or bag. Nez Perce (Plateau). This was probably produced after *circa* 1880; realistic figures of this type were relatively rare.
8 Horse being killed by a lance. From Lone Dog's (Sioux, Great Plains) winter count for 1824–25. This commemorates the event of Swan, a chief of the Two-Kettle tribe (a Teton Sioux sub-tribe) who had all of his horses killed.
9 Spotted horses. From Lone Dog's (Sioux, Great Plains) winter count for 1841–42. This commemorates a successful capturing of thirty horses by the Sioux (probably from the Crow). The spots are shown in red to distinguish them from those of a curly haired horse.

Chapter 4 – Southwest

page 38 Motifs on early Mogollon pottery bowl. The decorative workmanship from a tribe who occupied southwestern New Mexico from about AD900 to 1200, has been described as 'in a class all by itself'.

page 44 An animal motif of the type found on some of the finer types of early pottery from the Mimbres region of New Mexico and probably dating from before AD1100.

Chapter 5 – Plateau and Basin

page 52 *See above* – Introduction, page 7, number 7 and page 7, number 3.

page 53 A stepped decorative motif as found in Yakima, Umatilla and Nez Perce basketry.

page 57 Decorative motifs used in Yakima, Umatilla and Nez Perce weaving. (*See also* Introduction, page 6, number 8).

Chapter 6 – Northwest Coast

page 62 A figure of a dog-fish tattooed on the back of a Haida Indian named *Makde'gos* (who himself was a master tattooer), from Queen Charlotte Islands, 1884.

page 63 A Thunderbird motif as used by the Makah and Nootka tribes. Thunderbirds figured prominently in Northwest Coast mythology.

Chapter 7 – California

page 68 A pictograph from the coastal Chumash culture and probably dating prior to AD1800. Human figures, as shown here, were generally of a strange shamanistic form.

Chapter 10 – Indians in the Twentieth Century

page 87 *See above* – Introduction, page 7, number 2.

PICTURE CREDITS

The author would like to thank numerous individuals and institutions in the United Kingdom, Canada and the United States for their permission and help with a number of the illustrations published in this volume. In particular, thanks to Bill Holm of Seattle for permission to use his superb painting, *Parade* (Frontispiece, page 2) and for the gifts of several exquisite vignettes which he has given to me over our many years of friendship; two of these are reproduced on the Half-title and Title pages (pages 1 and 3). Every effort has been made to trace and acknowledge the copyright holders who are as follows:

National Anthropological Archives, Smithsonian Institution, Washington: Cover, 8, 13, 23(2), 26(2), 36, 45, 47, 49, 51, 57, 59, 61, 62, 67, 68, 70, 73, 74, 78, 79, 81, 83(2). S. D. Nelson, Flagstaff, Arizona: 6, 11 (top). John Painter, Cincinnati, Ohio: 8 (top right), 9 (top right), 34 (bottom right). Private collection: 9, 60 (bottom right), 88 (top left). Carl Sun: 19, 50, 58, 60. National Bison Range, Boise: 19. Hastings Museum and Art Gallery (Blackmore Collection), Hastings, East Sussex: 21 (bottom right), 60 (top right), 63 (top right), 82 (top right), 90 (right). Sam Cahoon, New Jersey: 29 (left). Royal British Columbia Museum (Courtesy, Dan Savard): 64. St. Francis Xavier Mission, Kahnawake, Quebec (Courtesy, Father Cyr Louis): 86. John A. Day, Vermillion, South Dakota (and Heidi Howe): 89. Judge L. Piersol, Sioux Falls, South Dakota: 90. Scott Bear Don't Walk, Billings, Montana: 92. Barbara Feezor-Stewart: 92. George R. Hamell, New York State Museum, Albany: 92. Niki Sandnal, Washington: 93. Gary J. Thibeault, Photographic Coordinator, Foxwoods Resort Casino: 93. University of California: 69 (top right).
All other images are from the Taylor Archives and Collection.

SUGGESTED FURTHER READING

The literature on the North American Indian is extensive. The titles below are suggested as a mixture of the 'popular', historical and scientific and most have bibliographies which can suggest further reading.

Adney, Edwin Tappan & Chapelle, Howard I. *The Bark Canoes and Skin Boats of North America*, Museum of History & Technology, Smithsonian Institution, Washington D.C. 1964.
Amsden, Charles Avery *Navaho Weaving: Its Technic and its History*, The Rio Grande Press Inc., Glorieta, New Mexico. I934.
Bahti, Tom *Southwestern Indian Tribes*, KC Publication, Flagstaff. 1968.
Brody, Hugh *Living Arctic: Hunters of the Canadian North*, Douglas & McIntyre, Vancouver. 1987.
Brown, Joseph Epes (ed.) *The Sacred Pipe: Black Elk's Account of the Seven Rites of the Oglala Sioux*, The Penguin Metaphysical Library, Harmondsworth, Middlesex. 1971.
Catlin, George *Letters and Notes on the Manners, Customs, and Condition of the North American Indians*, 2 Vols. Egyptian Hall, Piccadilly, London. 1841.
Cleland, Charles E. *Art of the Great Lakes Indians*, Flint Institute of Arts, Flint, Michigan. 1973.
Cook, Sherburn F. *The Conflict Between the California Indians and White Civilization*, University of California Press, Berkeley. 1976.
Culin, Stewart *Games of the North American Indians*, (1907). Reprint: Dover Publications, New York. 1975.
Ewers, John C. *The Horse in Blackfoot Indian Culture*, Bull.159. Bureau of American Ethnology, Smithsonian Institution, Washington D.C. 1955.
Plains Indian Painting, Stanford University Press, Stanford University, California. 1939.
Farabee, William C. *Indian Cradles*, Museum Journal No. 11:4 University of Pennsylvania, Philadelphia 1920.
Feder, Norman *American Indian Art*, Harry N. Abrams, Inc., New York. 1965.
Feest, Christian F. *Native Arts of North America*, Oxford University Press, New York & Toronto. 1980.
Ferg, Alan (ed.) *Western Apache Material Culture: The Goodwin and Guenther Collections*, The University of Arizona Press, Tucson, Arizona. 1987.
Garbarino, Merwyn S. *The Seminole*, Chelsea House Publishers, New York & Philadelphia. 1989.
Gilman, Carolyn & Schneider, Mary Jane *The Way to Independence*, Minnesota Historical Society Press, St. Paul. 1987.
Green, Rayna *Women in American Indian Society*, Edited by Frank W. Porter III. Chelsea House Publishers, New York & Philadelphia. 1992.
Grinnell, George Bird *The Cheyenne Indians: Their History and Ways of Life*, 2 Vols. Yale University: Press, New Haven. 1923.
Hail, Barbara A. & Duncan, Kate C. *Out of the North*, Haffenreffer Museum of Anthropology, Brown University, Bristol, Rhode Island. 1989.
Hamilton, T. M. *Native American Bows*, Appendix by Bill Holm. Missouri Archaeological Society, Special Publications No. 5, Columbia, Missouri. 1982.
Johnson, Michael G. *The Native Tribes of North America*, Macmillan Publishing Company, New York and Maxwell Macmillan Canada, Toronto. 1994.
Jonaitis, Aldona *From the Land of the Totem Poles*, American Museum of Natural History, New York and British Museum Publications, London. 1988.
Kroeber, Alfred L. *Handbook of the Indians of California*, Reprint: California Book Company Ltd., Berkeley. 1970.
Kroeber, Theodora *Ishi In Two Worlds: A Biography of the Last Wild Indian in North America*, The Cresset Library, London. Reprint. 1987.
Laubin, Reginald & Gladys *The Indian Tipi*, University of Oklahoma Press, Norman, Oklahoma. 1957.
Lewis, Meriwether & Clark, William *The History of the Lewis and Clark Expedition*, Edited by Elliott Coues. 1893. Reprint: Dover Publications Inc., New York.
McCary, Ben C. *Indians in Seventeenth-Century Virginia*, The University Press of Virginia, Charlottesville. 1957.
Mooney, James *The Ghost Dance Religion and Wounded Knee*, 14th Annual Report of the Bureau of American Ethnology, Smithsonian Institution, Washington D.C. 1896.
Ray, Arthur J. *Indians in the Fur Trade: their role as hunters, trappers and middlemen in the lands southwest of Hudson Bay 1660–1870*, University of Toronto Press, Toronto and Buffalo. 1974.
Sturtevant, William C. & Taylor, Colin F. *The Native Americans*, Salamander Books Ltd., London. 1991.
Tanner, Clara Lee *Prehistoric Southwestern Craft Arts*, The University of Arizona Press, Tucson, Arizona. 1976.
Taylor, Colin F. *The Plains Indians*, Salamander Books Ltd., London. 1994.
Native American Myths and Legends, (Ed.). Salamander Books Ltd., London. I994.
Native American Arts and Crafts, (Ed.). Salamander Books Ltd, London. 1995.
Myths of the North American Indians, Calmann and King Ltd., London. 1995.
Native American Life, Salamander Books Ltd., London 1996.
Wapa'ha:The Plains Feathered Head-dress (Die Plains Federhaube). Bilingual (English/German). Verlag fur Amerikanistk Wyk auf Foehr, Germany (2nd Edition). 1996.
Catlin's O-kee-pa: Mandan Culture and Ceremonialism. The George Catlin O-kee-pa Manuscript in the British Museum, Foreword by W. Raymond Wood. Bilingual (English/German). Verlag fur Amerikanistik, Wyk auf Foehr. Germany. 1996.
Turner, Geoffrey *Hair Embroidery in Siberia and North America*, Edited by T.K.Penniman & B.M. Blackwood. Occasional Papers on Technology 7. Pitt Rivers Museum, University of Oxford, Oxford. 1955.
West, Ian *Portraits of Native Americans*, Salamander Books Ltd., London. 1995.
Whiteford, Andrew Hunter *Southwestern Indian Baskets: Their History and Their Makers*, School of American Research Press, Santa Fe, New Mexico. 1988.
Whitehead, Ruth Holmes *Micmac Quillwork*, The Nova Scotia Museum, Halifax, Nova Scotia, 1982.